HOW TO GUIDE
GIRL SCOUT JUNIORS THROUGH

aMUSE

IT'S YOUR STORY—TELL IT! *A LEADERSHIP JOURNEY*

Girl Scouts of the USA

girl scouts

CHAIR,
NATIONAL BOARD
OF DIRECTORS
Kathy Hopinkah Hannan

CHIEF
EXECUTIVE
OFFICER
Anna Maria Chávez

CHIEF OPERATING
OFFICER
Jan Verhage

VICE PRESIDENT,
PROGRAM
Eileen Doyle

SENIOR DIRECTOR, PROGRAM RESOURCES Suzanne Harper
ART DIRECTOR: Douglas Bantz
WRITERS: Joan Nichols, Valerie Takahama,
Andrea Bastiani Archibald, Frankie Wright
EXECUTIVE EDITOR: Laura J. Tuchman
ILLUSTRATORS: Meghan Eplett, Helen Dardik, Jing Jing Tsong
DESIGNER: Rocco Alberico
PROGRAM TEAM: Ellen Kelliher, Sarah Micklem,
Sheryl O'Connell, Lesley Williams

© 2010 by Girl Scouts of the USA

First published in 2010 by Girl Scouts of the USA
420 Fifth Avenue, New York, NY 10018-2798
www.girlscouts.org

ISBN: 978-0-88441-757-6

the dove self-esteem fund

This publication was made
possible by a generous grant
from the Dove Self-Esteem Fund.

PHOTOGRAPHS: Pages 78 & 79, images of pins used with permission from *Read My Pins: Stories
from a Diplomat's Jewel Box*, by Madeleine K. Albright, HarperCollins Publishers, photographs by
John Bigelow Taylor; Page 81, Margaret Bourke-White/Time & Life Pictures/Getty Images

The women mentioned in this book are examples of how women have used their voice in the world. This
doesn't mean that GSUSA (or you) will agree with everything they have ever done or said.

STATEMENT OF TRUST

Girl Scouts of the USA creates national program materials to serve our
vast and diverse community of girls. To help bring topics "off the page
and into life," we sometimes provide girls—and their volunteers—with
suggestions about what people across the country and around the world are
doing, as well as movies, books, music, web pages, and more that might
spark girl interest.

At Girl Scouts of the USA, we know that not every example or suggestion
we provide will work for every girl, family, volunteer, or community.

In partnership with those who assist you with your Girl Scout group, including
parents, faith groups, schools, and community organizations, we trust you
to choose "real life topic experts" from your community, as well as movies,
books, music, websites and other opportunities that are most appropriate
for the girls in your area and that will enrich their Girl Scout activities.

Thank you for all you do to bring the Girl Scout Leadership Experience
to life with girls, so that they become leaders in their own lives—and the
future leaders the world needs!

CONTENTS

Building girls' **confidence**

is the goal of this *It's Your Story—Tell It!* journey.

Building **confidence** every day.

Girl Scouting builds girls of **courage**, **confidence**, and character, who make the world a better place.

That's our **mission.** And we do it through 3 keys to leadership: **Discover + Connect + Take Action**

On this journey...

Girl Scout Juniors try on whatever roles they choose for themselves.

Then they get creative—in any way they like! They tell stories and inspire others to try on new roles, too.

Trying on roles and realizing their limitless potential— that builds confidence!

Imagine how far a Junior can go and how much she can do—for herself *and* the world—when she has confidence.

Now, multiply that confidence by 564,000, the number of Girl Scout Juniors in the world. Those Juniors will be leaders in their own lives and leaders in the world—because they Discover, Connect, and Take Action. That's a future to journey toward!

What to pack for the journey!

Girl Scout leadership journeys invite girls to explore a theme through many experiences and from many perspectives—through the 3 keys to leadership: **Discover + Connect + Take Action**

All the joys of travel are built right in! So fill your suitcase with everything you need for an amazing trip that will change girls' lives!

The Girls' Book

Exciting roles and activities, real-life stories, and creative projects let girls . . . meet new people, explore new things, make memories, earn badges, and have fun— all while exploring a theme through the 3 keys to leadership!!

The Adult Guide

Fun and easy activities to get girls thinking and doing while team-building and getting creative—all the while exploring the 3 keys to leadership! Plus: healthful snacks and loads of tips for engaging girls in leadership.

Your Wider Community

Women in all career fields, and experts in storytelling and the arts. Local partners: museums, arts groups, professional associations, colleges, and libraries.

Your Enthusiasm

. . . and your interests and talents, your partnership with girls and families, and, most important, your willingness to learn by doing, right alongside the girls!

Stories + = 2 Fun Ways
Trying on Roles
to Build Girls' Leadership

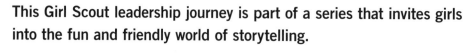

This Girl Scout leadership journey is part of a series that invites girls into the fun and friendly world of storytelling.

Stories are fundamental to how girls learn about themselves and the world.

Stories allow girls to absorb the ideas and richness of many cultures, and that develops their empathy, tolerance, and acceptance of others.

Stories sharpen girls' minds and spark their imaginations.

Stories inspire and motivate.

Stories teach girls how to lead and keep them growing as leaders.

Inspiring Stories! Along the journey, girls find that telling stories and taking on roles through dance, drawing, drama—or whatever way they choose—can be so much fun. No wonder it's called "playing" a role!

Stories about roles

Girls read inspiring stories of real women who have taken on such roles as playwright, costume designer, dancer, and chef, and some who have busted stereotypes by becoming the first female Secretary of State or a champion long-distance swimmer.

Girls expand their own stories by trying on roles

Girls keep logs of all the roles they play in life and the roles of women and girls around them. Then they try out even more roles! Plus, a comic story in their book lets them decide what happens when characters try on new roles!

A book for every girl!
So that girls can enjoy the journey whenever they like, it's important that all girls have their own journey book. They can draw inspiration from the book and add their personal inspirations to it! This book may become their own journey journal—and one of the many mementos the girls will cherish throughout their years in Girl Scouting and beyond!

All the Journey's a Stage!

This journey's theme of trying on roles lends itself to all sorts of associations with theater. So along this journey, the **Juniors** have fun with a variety of acting-themed activities that give them an opportunity to express themselves and get their creativity flowing! What could be better for building a positive sense of self? Here's a peek:

1. Team Prop Box

This team effort stores props that remind the girls of all the roles they can play in life. The Juniors dip into it from time to time to try on new roles. The girls might choose to share the prop box with guests at the journey's final celebration or present it to a group of Brownies bridging to Juniors as an invitation to enjoy aMUSE, too! See page 32.

2. Wacky Warm Up
This tongue-twisting actors' exercise lets girls loosen up and sharpen their speaking skills before telling their story to an audience. See page 76.

3. Take the Stage
This charades-like game has each Junior jumping into the "spotlight" to act out a role as the other girls guess what role she is playing. See page 31.

4. Crazy Curtain Calls
Girls get active and have fun taking turns taking a bow and then being silly by throwing kisses, jumping up and down, or any action of their choice. See page 75.

Fun extras for the journey!

Family kickoff event Consider starting this journey with a family event where everyone joins in to decorate the Team Prop Box. See page 30.

Make-believe microphone using a toilet paper tube, aluminum foil, and ribbon that the girls can make and use during "acting" activities.

aMUSE-ing accessories for the girls to make and wear, such as pins fashioned from bottle caps or other recycled materials, and decorated with ribbon, sequins, glitter, and other craft materials.

Miniature muses, made using whatever art supplies are on hand, can remind the girls of what inspires them and how they inspire others, too!

Get out and see a performance! It doesn't have to be professional theater. Look around for a high school or college drama club production. The girls will love seeing older students take on a variety of roles on stage!

Why Self-Esteem Matters!

Health

Happiness

Athletic Ability

High self-esteem is linked to confidence and other positive benefits for girls . . .

Academic Achievement

Social Skills

Self-esteem means how a girl feels about herself—her abilities, her body, her capacity to seek and meet challenges in the world. On average, the self-esteem of Junior-age girls is relatively high. Keeping the Juniors' self-esteem high is one of the goals of this journey. That way, as the girls grow, they're more likely to avoid the drop in self-esteem that is so typical in adolescence. Without that drop, their confidence can soar!

Session Plans Make the Most of Juniors' Skills

The Sample Session plans starting on page 28 offer opportunities for the girls to enhance their skills and develop new ones while taking into account the abilities and needs of Junior-age girls. When planning additional creative adventures, be aware that fourth- and fifth-graders:

want to make decisions and express their opinions.	*So allow them to do so frequently through guided discussions and active reflection activities.*
are social and enjoy doing things in groups.	*So allow them to team up in small or large groups for art projects, performances, and written activities.*
are sensitive to the expectations and judgments of others.	*So share your own mistakes and learnings, and create an environment where girls can be comfortable sharing theirs.*
are concerned about equity and fairness.	*So don't shy away from discussing why rules are made and laws are passed, and have them develop their own for their group.*
are increasingly capable of critical thinking and can consider the perspectives of others.	*So assist them in developing these skills by asking them to explain their decisions, share their visions for their roles in the future, and appropriately challenge their own and others' perspectives.*
have strong fine and gross motor skills and coordination.	*So engage them in moving their minds and their bodies! Allow them to express themselves through the written word and choreography.*
love to write plays, create music, and dance.	*So they might like to tell a story through playwriting, playing an instrument, or sharing a song or dance.*
may be starting puberty.	*So be sensitive to girls' needs to adjust to their changing bodies and create an environment that celebrates this transition.*

Promoting Well-Being Along the Journey

Girl Scouting is guided by a positive philosophy of inclusion that benefits all. On this journey, especially, it is hoped that girls will increase their feelings of being powerful, capable, and strong as they enhance their skills and develop new ones. So, as the Girl Scout Law says, "be a sister to every Girl Scout." Determine whether any girls are new to town, are differently abled, don't speak English as a first language, or have parents who are getting a divorce. What counts most is being open-minded and aware, staying flexible, and creatively varying your approach with the girls.

3 Leadership Awards

IF A GIRL MISSES AN AWARD STEP . . .

Find a way for her to do something similar to what she missed so she can still earn the award with her group. Your goal is to guide her to have the same learning and growing opportunity—and to understand how she can contribute to the team. You might ask all the Juniors to brainstorm about how girls who miss steps can get back on track with the journey.

Girls may not experience activities in exactly the same way, but they can each take away new insights, connections, and a sense of accomplishment.

On this journey, the Juniors have the opportunity to earn three Girl Scout Leadership awards, all of which build foundational leadership skills critical to moving up the Girl Scout ladder of leadership and becoming lifelong leaders.

Reach Out!

What it means for Juniors: They understand the many roles women and girls play in the world around them and the leadership skills used to play them.

How Juniors: earn it: They keep a Casting Call Log and do an interview or a panel discussion (Sessions 1–4)

When Juniors: receive it: Session 4

Speak Out!

What it means for Juniors: They are aware of how stereotypes could hold themselves and others back from trying on roles, and they Take Action to help stop stereotypes.

How Juniors: earn it: They complete three Speak Out! activities, and team up to choose a stereotype and create and tell a story to help stop it (Sessions 5-8).

When Juniors receive it: Session 8

Try Out!

What it means for Juniors: They have the courage and confidence to try out new roles.

How Juniors: earn it: They keep a Role Call Log and choose and complete two other Try Out! activities (Sessions 9-10).

When Juniors: receive it: Final Celebration

LADDER OF LEADERSHIP

As Girl Scouts take journeys and earn the awards, they're
climbing a ladder that lets them be leaders
in their own lives and in the world! Pass it on!

It's Your World—Change It!

Ambassadors raise their voices to advocate for issues they care about.

Seniors learn that leaders have a vision and can move the world a step closer to it.

Cadettes develop the people skills that leaders need.

Juniors learn that leaders need power—their own, their team's, and their community's.

Brownies go on a quest to find the three keys to leadership.

Daisies have fun—and learn leadership skills—in the garden.

It's Your Story—Tell It!

Girls move dreams forward!

AMBASSADOR

Girls see how much sisterhood does for the world!

SENIOR

Girls put the ME in media.

CADETTE

Girls explore all the roles open to them in life.

JUNIOR

Girls explore their place in the wide world of girls.

BROWNIE

Girls learn they can care for animals and themselves.

DAISY

It's Your Planet—Love It!

Ambassadors learn that leaders aim for justice.

Seniors find out what leaders can sow for Earth.

Cadettes become leaders in clearing the air!

Juniors bring energy solutions to the world.

Brownies take the lead in saving Earth's water.

Daisies learn to protect Earth's treasures.

What You'll Find in Each Sample Session Plan

Journey activities are sequenced to give girls lots of fun and exciting challenges centered around earning the journey's three leadership awards. But don't feel you and the girls must do everything in the Sample Sessions or in the order given. Think of journey activities as pieces that can be mixed, matched, and coordinated according to the needs of your group of Juniors.

THE JOURNEY SNAPSHOT gives an overview of what's ahead

AT A GLANCE gives the session's goal, activities, and recommended materials.

TOWARD THE AWARD ICONS indicate activities that step girls toward a leadership award.

CEREMONIES, opening and closing, mark the Juniors' time together as special.

ACTIVE TIME
activities get girls moving!

WHAT TO SAY
A full script for you to use! Must you follow it? No! Let it guide you, but be yourself!

CREATIVE ACTIVITIES
encourage creativity, self-expression and teamwork.

SNACKS
offer girls healthful, and *aMUSE*-ing, energy boosters.

OPTION: MINGLING AMONG FRIENDS
If the girls in the group already know each other, try this variation. After the leader shouts "Freeze," the girl who gets pointed to calls out the name of the girl opposite her in the circle, and names one thing she knows about her.

Time to Mingle
Keep the girls active with this version of the vocal warm-ups that actors do to loosen up before they rehearse or perform. Here, the girls learn more about one another and their roles in daily life. You might say something like:

What we are about to do might seem really silly, but it's something actors like to do to loosen up before a performance.

Ask for a girl volunteer to be the leader, and then get them playing the game by offering these directions:

- Start by walking in a circle, and mumbling, "mingle, mingle, mingle . . . ," as you go. Try to face one another as you walk so you're not just looking at your feet or the back of the girl in front of you.
- Keep walking and mumbling "mingle" until the leader shouts, "Freeze!"
- When "Freeze" is called, stop and face the girl opposite you across the circle. Then the leader points to one of you. If the leader points to you, call out your name and one thing about yourself. "My name is _____ and _____" ("I love dogs," "I play guitar," "I'm building a robot").
- Then the leader points to the girl across the circle. She repeats what the first girl said, but in a tone the leader decides, such as "happily," "very tired," "rushed," "boldly," "like you are very curious," "whiny," "like you have a cold," "angrily," "giggly, like a little kid," "formally, like a president," and so forth.
- Then another girl will volunteer to lead the group, and you'll all start again walking and mumbling, "Mingle, mingle." We'll wrap up when you've all had a chance to be the leader and everyone has had a chance to speak.

Then you might ask the girls what they noticed about trying on different roles and attitudes by changing their tone of voice. Try some questions like these:

- What roles and voices did you like? Which were your favorites?
- Which didn't you feel comfortable with? Why?

Toward the Award: Logs and Leaders
Ask the girls to turn to the Casting Call Log on page 16 of their book, and let them know that filling it out is a step toward their Reach Out! Award. Explain that the log is a place to list all the women they meet in their daily lives and the roles they play. Say something like:

- At the end of our last session, I asked you to be on the lookout for all the roles girls and women play in your life. Think about the past few days—and all the women you saw—at home, on the way to school, in the halls, in class, at lunch, after school.
- In your Casting Call Log, write down who you saw and the roles they were playing.
- If you don't know their names, write their roles. If there are just too many, write a few for now. You can fill in the rest later.

Page 16, girls' book

Take a few moments for the girls to share their lists with one another. Then get a discussion going with questions like:

team talk!

- How many roles are you seeing the women in your life play?
- Which of these women play more than one role? What are they?
- Which of these women do you consider leaders, either in their own life or in the community? Why?
- What leadership traits do you see in them that you also see in yourself?
- Which leadership traits do you see in them that you aspire to?
- Now, think about the Girl Scout Law and all the values in it. Which of those values do these women seem to honor in the roles they play?
- Which of these values do you also honor?
- Which roles played by these women would you like to try?

Congratulate the girls on getting started with their logs, and taking a step toward earning their Reach Out! Award. Encourage them to keep filling out their logs as they see more women and girls in their daily lives, and let them know they'll share the logs again when they get together next time.

KEEP DISCUSSIONS FREE FLOWING
These and other suggested discussion questions are just that: suggestions. Feel free to omit some or add in others of your own, and let the conversations go where the girls take them.

And if you need to get the discussion about women and their roles going, offer a few roles that you have noticed. Example: the woman who delivers my mail, the veterinarian who cares for my cat.

best friend writer chef tech whiz
poet fashion stylist athlete yoga

36 37

Quick Draw
Hand out drawing paper, pencils, and erasers and let the girls know they are about to try a fun way to find out how they picture various roles in life. You might say, *I am going to call out roles and you have one minute to draw the first picture that comes to mind.* Let them know that just a quick sketch is needed—even a stick figure is fine!

Possible roles: tennis player, newscaster, farmer, model, dentist, dancer, mayor, doctor, nurse, grocer, waiter, flight attendant, pilot, golfer, basketball player, firefighter, police officer, president, skier, bike racer, mail carrier, banker, pet shop owner, veterinarian, gym teacher, science teacher, librarian, secretary, math teacher, English teacher, college student, scientist, scuba diver.

Now get the girls talking about who they see on TV or in the movies in those roles, whether they are mostly males or females, and how what they see may have affected why they see certain roles. You might ask:

- Why do you think you drew that role as a woman (or man)?
- Do you know someone who plays that role in real life? Or do you see someone on TV or in the movies who plays that role? Do you ever base your ideas of what someone in a role is like by what you see on TV or in movies without meaning to?
- Could someone older (or younger) play that role, too?

QUICK DRAW, PART 2: QUICK-CHANGE ARTIST!
Call out one of the characteristics listed below and ask the girls to erase and change one of their drawings to be the opposite of what it now is. Point out that these attributes are some of the ones that people might unthinkingly use to limit a person's roles, and that being one way or the other shouldn't stop people from trying out roles. For example, if the girls drew a male dentist and you call out "gender," they erase and change the dentist's hair and face to be female because both women and men can be dentists. Do as many rounds of "Quick-Change Artist!" as the girls like, using these prompts:

- Gender (male/female)
- Age (young/old)
- Size (short/tall; large/small)

STEREOTYPES = LIMITED ROLES
To help the girls understand what stereotypes are, you might say something like:

Think about how, in our own minds, we sometimes limit the roles that people in the world can play.

For example, you might not think of your dad as someone who would braid your hair or help you pick out a party dress. Or you might think that [that's] who's really [...] would [...]

[...] all the roles [...] can play—even [...] of our minds—we put people in a role we choose for them, rather than a role they choose for themselves. That's what we call stereotyping!

As the discuss stereotypes, add in even more examples that you are aware of—and encourage the girls to do the same!

38

---

aMUSE-ing Snacks
QUICK-DRAW, OPEN-FACE SANDWICHES
Invite the girls to have some fun "drawing" creatively (with the pesto or fruit or vegetable purees or sauces—whatever the girls decided) on whole-grain rice cakes or bread. The sauces can be applied with small kitchen brushes or they can be placed in squeeze bottles, with which the girls can easily "draw." What the girls choose to "draw" is up to them!

Role-Play Switcheroo
Without realizing it, the Juniors may be playing out stereotypical gender roles in their daily lives. To make the girls more conscious of stereotypes, invite them to take turns role-playing girls and boys in a classroom situation. The roles to play: one teacher and an even number of girl and boy students.

Let the girls choose whether they want to be "girl" students and wear sticky notes with blue dots, or "boy" students and wear red dots. Encourage them to divide into equal numbers of "girls" and "boys." Ask for a volunteer who will play the teacher, who might be male or female, and for suggestions from the Juniors on the topic of the day's lesson—something in math, science, language arts, or current events, for example—which should be something they've studied in school and know fairly well.

Invite the girls to act out a typical class scenario, with the "teacher" standing in front, asking questions and encouraging discussion. Halfway through the role-play, ask "girls" and "boys" to switch stickies and roles. After the role-play, encourage the girls to discuss what happened. You can guide the discussion with such questions as:

- Who put their hands up the most, "boys" or "girls"?
- Who offered their opinions the most?
- Who disrupted most, "boys" or "girls"?
- How did being a "boy" or a "girl" make you feel or act differently?
- Is there anything you now want to change about how you act in class? If yes, what? Why?

Creating a Network of Journey Resources

GO ONLINE FOR LETTERS HOME

Visit the Journeys section of girlscouts.org for letters and forms to start your Friends and Family Network and keep its members informed and motivated to join in all the fun the Juniors will have on this journey! You'll find:

- Ideas for reaching out to local arts experts and other resources
- Checklist for Friends and Family Network

You'll get a break and expand the girls' awareness of community by asking family members, friends, and friends of friends to visit and enhance the Juniors' gatherings. So go ahead and "hand off" activities and prep steps to a Friends and Family Network. Here are some tips:

- Before the journey begins, aim for a brief get-together (even online!) with the girls, their parents, caregivers, relatives, and friends.

- Find out who likes to do what, identify assistants for various activities, and see who has time for behind-the-scenes preparations, gathering supplies (pads, markers, glitter, glue), or snack duty.

- Keep in mind that in some families, an aunt, older sibling, cousin, or other adult may be most able to participate.

More Print and Online Journey Resources

☐ **Girl Scout Safety Activity Checkpoints** detail the safety net provided for girls in Girl Scouting. Seek them out from your council and keep them handy!

☐ **It's Your Journey—Customize It!** is your guide to making the most of Girl Scout leadership journeys.

☐ **Volunteer Essentials** is your guide to all things Girl Scouts! Seek it out from your council.

JUNIOR JOURNEY PEOPLE POWER

FRIENDS & FAMILY NETWORK: Name	Willing to help with:	Phone and e-mail address

COUNCIL CONTACTS: Name	Willing to help with:	Phone and e-mail address

LOCAL EXPERTS: Name	Area of expertise	Phone and e-mail address

Girl Scout Traditions and Ceremonies

GIRL SCOUT DAYS TO CELEBRATE

- **Founder's Day**
  October 31
  Juliette "Daisy" Gordon Low's birthday

- **World Thinking Day**
  February 22
  A day for Girl Scouts and Girl Guides throughout the world to think about one another

- **Girl Scout Birthday**
  March 12
  The day in 1912 when Juliette Gordon Low officially registered the organization's first 18 girl members in Savannah, Georgia

Traditions and ceremonies have always been part of the fun of being a Girl Scout. They show girls they are part of a sisterhood: They connect girls to one another, to their sister Girl Scouts and Girl Guides around the world, and to the generations of girls who were Girl Scouts before them.

A few traditions are mentioned here; your council will have many more. Try incorporating them into Girl Scout gatherings and get-togethers. And be sure to involve the girls in creating and passing on new traditions.

THE GIRL SCOUT SIGN

The Girl Scout sign is made when saying the Girl Scout Promise. It is formed by holding down the thumb and little finger on the right hand and leaving the three middle fingers extended (these three fingers represent the three parts of the Promise).

THE GIRL SCOUT HANDSHAKE

The Girl Scout handshake is the way many Girl Guides and Girl Scouts greet each other. They shake their left hands while making the Girl Scout sign with their right hand. The left-handed handshake represents friendship because the left hand is closer to the heart than the right.

WIDENING THE FRIENDSHIP CIRCLE

The Friendship Circle and friendship squeeze are often used as a closing ceremony for meetings and campfires. Everyone gathers in a circle, crosses their right arm over their left, and holds hands with the people on either side. Once everyone is silent, one girl starts the friendship squeeze by squeezing the hand of the person to the left. One by one, each girl passes on the squeeze until it travels around the circle.

Since this journey emphasizes learning about and trying on new roles, encourage the girls to widen their circle from time to time by inviting teens or adults to their opening or closing ceremonies to share the many roles they play in their lives.

ENCOURAGE THE GIRLS TO CUSTOMIZE, AND ADD SURPRISE

As the Juniors decide how to customize their journey (see page 32) to create the most meaningful experience for their group, encourage them to go all out with ceremonies and traditions while also branching out to enjoy new adventures in their region. The girls might decide:

- Whether to celebrate earning their awards with small ceremonies throughout the journey or one big one at the end, with family, friends, and other invited guests

- Whether to plan trips to a storytelling festival or an art museum, or to a performance of a children's theater production or a concert

- Whether they want to have an outdoor adventure with stories around the campfire

- Whether they would like to tell a story in crafts by making individual prop boxes, a team scrapbook, or other projects

Keep all of these ideas in mind and add to them as you and the girls explore the journey's themes. Encourage the Juniors to create a new tradition whenever they like!

Keys to Girl Leadership

Girl Scouting prepares girls to be leaders—in their own daily lives and in the world around them. We do this through the Girl Scout Leadership Experience, pictured below, which is the basis for everything girls do in Girl Scouting. The three keys to leadership—Discover (self), Connect (team up and network with others), and Take Action (make a difference in the world)—are a shorthand way of capturing all of the 15 national leadership benefits girls get in Girl Scouting.

As you can see in the charts on pages 94–96, all of the experiences in this journey have been created to engage girls in exploring these three keys to leadership. In fact, that's what makes a Girl Scout journey so special: Everything girls and their adult guides need to explore the leadership keys is built right in! So all along the way, you will be guiding the Juniors toward leadership skills and qualities they can use right now—and all their lives. Keep in mind that the intended benefits to girls are the cumulative result of traveling through an entire journey—and everything else girls experience in Girl Scouting!

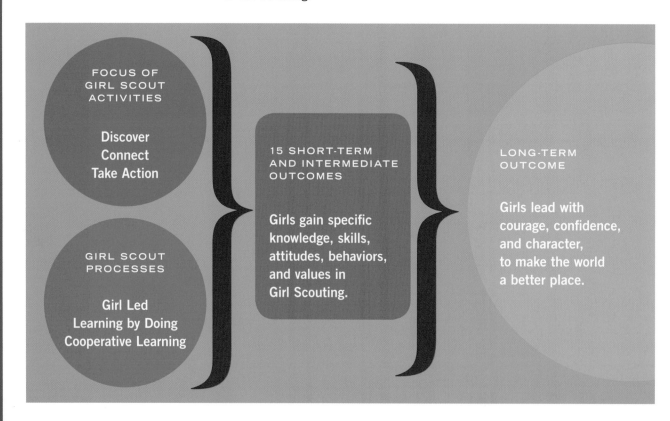

FOCUS OF
GIRL SCOUT
ACTIVITIES

Discover
Connect
Take Action

GIRL SCOUT
PROCESSES

Girl Led
Learning by Doing
Cooperative Learning

15 SHORT-TERM
AND INTERMEDIATE
OUTCOMES

Girls gain specific
knowledge, skills,
attitudes, behaviors,
and values in
Girl Scouting.

LONG-TERM
OUTCOME

Girls lead with
courage, confidence,
and character,
to make the world
a better place.

How Girls Have Fun in Girl Scouts

In Girl Scouting, girls enjoy activities based on the three keys to leadership and built on three processes that make Girl Scouting distinct from school and other extracurricular activities. The keys and processes are built right into the journey for you—in the Sample Session plans! So you know a little more about how the processes play out for Juniors, here's a quick summary:

Girl Led

Girl Led means girls play an active part in figuring out the what, where, when, how, and why of their activities. Encourage them to lead the planning, decision-making, learning, and fun as much as possible. This ensures that girls experience leadership opportunities as they prepare to become active participants in their communities. With Juniors, you could:

- encourage girls to plan and lead a session, activity, project, or event
- model and provide strategies for solving problems and making decisions
- expose girls to diverse ideas, geographies, and culture

Learning by Doing

Learning by Doing engages girls in continuous cycles of action and reflection that result in deeper understanding of concepts and mastery of skills. As they participate in activities and then reflect on them, girls explore their own questions, discover answers, gain new skills, and share ideas and observations. It's important for girls to connect their experiences to their lives and apply what they have learned to future experiences. With Juniors, you could:

- talk with the girls about ways to connect their learning to their daily life
- guide girls to reflect on their learning by using the many ideas in this journey
- support girls' hands-on testing of their own ideas, skill-building, and teaching skills

Cooperative Learning

Cooperative Learning has girls work together toward goals with mutual respect and collaboration. Working together in all-girl environments encourages girls to feel powerful and emotionally and physically safe, and allows them to experience a sense of belonging. With Juniors, you could:

- structure experiences so that girls "need" one another to complete tasks
- use role-play scenarios to guide girls in working effectively within groups
- give girls examples of how to assign roles within the group, assess how they are doing, and stay on task

---

KEEP IT GIRL LED

Remember: You want the girls to take a major role in planning and executing this leadership experience. The girls may first want you to come up with the ideas and plans. But hold your ground! This is the girls' experience, and they're up to the challenge!

From beginning to end, keep your eye on what the girls want to do and the direction they seem to be taking. It's the approach begun by Juliette Gordon Low: When she and her associates couldn't decide on a new direction, she often said, "Let's ask the girls!"

Girl Led experiences are built right into this journey to make it easy for you.

At each session, ask the girls for their own thoughts on what they've done or discussed.

What It All Means for Girls

All activities in this leadership journey relate to Discovering, Connecting, and Taking Action—the three Girl Scout keys to leadership! Plus, Girl Led, Cooperative Learning, and Learning by Doing processes make the activities fun and powerful for girls. Here, in an activity from Session 4, you can see how these processes and the national Girl Scout outcomes—the benefits we want for girls—play out during a team gathering. The processes and outcomes are so seamless you might not even notice them. Throughout the journey, processes and outcomes play out again and again. Before you know it, you'll be using these valuable aspects of Girl Scouting in whatever Juniors do!

FROM SAMPLE SESSION 4

Ads Assume . . .

Explain to the girls that advertising experts have the job of selecting pictures or photos to place in ads and on packaging for products designed for them, such as toys, games, or sports clothes and equipment. Executives of the company selling a product often make the final decision about which pictures or photos will do the best job of selling their products. Let the girls know that they will now play the role of those executives! Say something like,

How would you like to be an executive in charge of picking the pictures used to sell products to young people? You'll decide if the pictures are right for the ad or not.

Place the ads and packaging you and the girls have collected in the center of a table. Ask the girls to take turns choosing an item and placing it in one of three piles:

- Products for girls
- Products for boys
- Products for girls and boys

Ask the girls to say quickly whether they agree with the choices for each pile and if not, explain why. (Let them know they do not need to agree with one another, but they should listen respectfully to one another's views and feel comfortable speaking up to explain their own views.)

With the girls making the decisions about whether or not pictures are appropriate for the advertisement, this activity is **Girl Led** from the start. And, as they sort the advertisements into the different piles, girls are engaged in the **Learning by Doing** process.

When girls listen respectfully to one another and speak up for their own views, they are strengthening their healthy relationship (**Connect outcome, Girls develop healthy relationships**) and advocacy skills (**Take Action outcome, Girls advocate for themselves and others, locally and globally**) as well as advancing on the **Connect outcome, Girls promote cooperation and team building**.

Before the "executives" decide whether to accept or change the images, pose a few questions like these:

How would you describe the images you're seeing?

Who is shown using the product in these images? Who's simply looking on?

Are you seeing any stereotypes in these images?

How is it useful for advertisers to use stereotypical images in their ads?

When boys and girls are shown together, who is taller? Who looks older?

Which images seem to appeal most to girls? Which seem to appeal more to boys?

How does the image "make" you want to have the product it's about?

Do any girls or boys you know use this product? Do you know whether or not they like it?

Why might a boy or girl want or not want to use this product?

Now ask the girls to pile up any of the images or packaging they think need to be changed because they don't seem to represent a real view of the way girls or boys act in the world. Then invite them to use the art supplies on hand to alter the ads or packaging so that they do represent a real view of the world as they know it. They might . . .

- paste or draw new images over the existing ones

- cut up the images and rearrange them in a way that they think makes better sense

- write what they want the people in the images to be saying by creating their own cartoon balloons and filling them in

- rewrite the ad or packaging copy

These sample discussion questions get girls evaluating advertisements and listening to and considering one another's perspectives—both move girls forward on the **Discover outcome, Girls develop critical thinking**. And, depending on the advertisements chosen, these questions might also make girls more aware of cultural and media influences on their and other girls' ability to make healthy choices in their lives, which helps girls advance on the **Discover outcome, Girls gain practical life skills**—girls practice healthy living.

Girls get hands-on here as they alter the ads they have compiled and create new ads together. They are engaged in both the **learning by doing** and **cooperative learning** processes as they team up to develop more accurate "real world" images and advertising copy. As they develop these more realistic portrayals they might include images and words representative of diverse background, viewpoints, and life experiences. In this way, they are also working toward achievement of the **Connect outcome, Girls advance diversity in a multicultural world**.

23

Your Perspective on Leadership

The Girl Scout keys to leadership—Discover + Connect + Take Action—demonstrate that leadership happens from the inside out. Your thoughts, enthusiasm, and approach will influence the Juniors, so take a few minutes now—and throughout the journey—to apply the three "keys" of leadership to yourself.

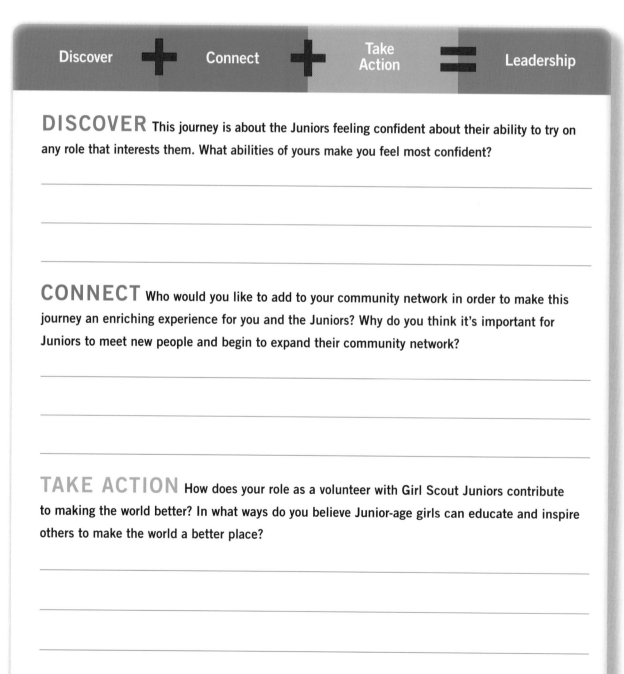

Discover + **Connect** + **Take Action** = **Leadership**

DISCOVER This journey is about the Juniors feeling confident about their ability to try on any role that interests them. What abilities of yours make you feel most confident?

_____

_____

_____

CONNECT Who would you like to add to your community network in order to make this journey an enriching experience for you and the Juniors? Why do you think it's important for Juniors to meet new people and begin to expand their community network?

_____

_____

_____

TAKE ACTION How does your role as a volunteer with Girl Scout Juniors contribute to making the world better? In what ways do you believe Junior-age girls can educate and inspire others to make the world a better place?

_____

_____

_____

....

....

....

....

....

....

....

....

....

....

....

....

....

....

....

....

....

....

....

Every session in this journey has been created to help girls become **confident leaders—** in their own lives and in the world!

How?

The journey gets girls using the **3 keys** to leadership: **Discover, Connect,** and **Take Action.**

Girls **Discover** themselves.

They **Connect** with others.

And they **Take Action** in the world!

And in every session of the journey, **girls lead, team up, and learn by doing.** (And you'll learn right along with them. Have a wonderful journey!)

For more on the leadership keys and Girl Scout processes and their benefits to girls, see pages 20–21 and 94–96 in this guide, and *Transforming Leadership: Focusing on Outcomes of the New Girl Scout Leadership Experience* (GSUSA, 2008) and *Transforming Leadership Continued* (GSUSA, 2009). Both publications are available on girlscouts.org.

JOURNEY SNAPSHOT

SESSION 1 Casting Call	The Juniors start thinking about all the roles available in the world for women and girls. They choose roles they'd like for themselves, play a game of charades of active roles for women, and make a Team Prop Box.
SESSION 2 Girls Can Be Anything!	The Juniors explore the many roles available to them and start to learn about stereotypes. They use a Casting Call Log to see what all the women around them are up to. They sketch how they picture various roles, and role-play stereotypical gender roles they might see in their lives.
SESSION 3 Callbacks	The Juniors reach out to women in their community to explore all the roles available to them. The girls add to their Casting Call Log, and plan to meet with some of the women from their log to learn more about what they do.
SESSION 4 Tell Us Your Story	The Juniors learn more about the roles women play in real life and in the media. The girls talk to the women they invited and explore ads for messages about roles girls and boys are asked to play. They earn their Reach Out! award.
SESSION 5 A Gathering of Storytellers	The Juniors team up to create an inspiring story about stereotypes that sends others a call to action for stopping stereotyping. They decide who can benefit most from hearing their story, and they choose a creative way to tell it.
SESSIONS 6 & 7 Our Muse, Your Project	The Juniors get busy turning their story into their chosen form of creative expression. The girls choose and practice the roles they will play when they present their story to educate and inspire an audience.
SESSION 8 Showtime!	The Juniors take the spotlight and tell their story. The girls ask their audience to pledge to join them in stopping stereotypes. The Juniors earn their Speak Out! award.
SESSION 9 Who I Am Now	The Juniors explore what beauty means to them, how they see it themselves, and how it informs their story. The girls use their imaginations to create self-portraits, and host an Arty Party to exhibit of their art work.
SESSION 10 Who I Might Be	The Juniors explore how having healthy bodies supports them in taking on roles, and how they can support and appreciate their bodies. The girls hold a dance party and plan their final celebration.
FINAL CELEBRATION Celebrating Me/ Celebrating Us	The Juniors celebrate their roles and accomplishments along the journey and gain the courage to continue trying on new roles throughout life. They earn their Try Out! award.

Acting out different roles kicks off the journey with a confidence boost!

CASTING CALL

SAMPLE SESSION 1
Casting Call

A ROUSING BEGINNING

Activities in this session launch the journey's two intertwining themes: trying on roles and the power of stories.

You might set up this first gathering as a special journey kickoff where artists from the community share their work with the girls. You might also invite your Friends and Family Network. Then everyone can start the journey together in a creative and exciting way!

AT A GLANCE

Goal: The Juniors have fun getting to know all the roles available in the world for women and girls.

- Opening Ceremony: Flurry of Roles

- Artists' Presentations (if local artists are invited)

- Take the Stage

- Inside the Prop Box

- Customizing the Journey

- *aMUSE*-ing Snacks: Sandwich "Role"-Ups

- Closing Ceremony: Roles and More Roles!

MATERIALS

- **Opening Ceremony: Flurry of Roles:** pre-prepared sticky notes (see "Roles to Use" sidebar on opposite page)

- **Artists' Presentations (if artists invited):** art stations, as needed

- **Take the Stage:** hat or bag, preprepared slips of paper

(see page 31)

- **Inside the Prop Box:** large box, art supplies (magazines, craft paper, fabric, beads, yarns, acrylic or any quick-drying paint, craft glue, markers)

- *aMUSE*-ing Snacks: see page 32

Pages 10–11, girls' book

PREPARE AHEAD

- For the Opening Ceremony, write the suggested roles (see page 29) on sticky notes and then place the notes on a wall or table where the girls can grab them. Make enough notes so each girl can have one of each role.

- For "Take the Stage," write the suggested "active" roles (see page 31) on slips of paper and then place them in a bag, hat, or other container.

- If artists are attending, have each one set up her "creation station" so the girls can view the art and then try creating something in that style or medium. Also call on your Network for art supplies and snack ingredients.

Opening Ceremony: Flurry of Roles

Gather the girls around the table (or wall) with the sticky notes and explain that each note names one of the many roles girls and women can play in life. Say:

- *When I call "Start!" you all have exactly one minute to grab some roles and stick them on yourselves and one another.*

- *Place only those roles you think are truly a good fit for yourself or whomever else you're placing them on.*

- *When I call "Time!" your minute is up.*

When the minute ends, bring the girls together, asking them not to remove any of their sticky notes. Then give them a moment or two to look at all the roles stuck to them. If some sticky notes are on their backs or elsewhere where they can't be seen, have other girls move them to where they'll be visible. Then ask:

**ROLES TO USE
(ADD YOUR OWN!)**

athlete, pilot, lawyer, veterinarian, news reporter, princess-in-training, artist, dancer, scientist, insect expert, ice skater, songwriter, astronaut, cartoonist, artist, surgeon, dolphin trainer, world traveler, writer, skydiver, businesswoman, friend, inventor, actor, leader of a band, chef, fashion stylist, game creator, coach

What do you think about the roles you chose for yourself? The roles other girls chose for you?

What about the roles you gave other girls?

Which roles do you think are the best fit for you? Which aren't a good fit at all? Why?

Which roles weren't chosen by anyone? Why do you think that is? Are they roles you never imagined trying? Why? Because you're a girl? Because you're a fourth-grader or a fifth-grader?

INTRODUCING THE JOURNEY'S THEMES

Then introduce the journey and its themes. You might say something like:

- *Today we're starting on a journey called* aMUSE. *On this journey, you'll explore all the roles available for women and girls. You'll imagine, create, and try out new roles for yourselves. You'll also encourage others to try new roles.*

- *Student and Girl Scout are roles you play right now. What are some others? You may also be a computer whiz, soccer player, friend, pet lover, dancer, reader, writer—the list may seem endless! So it's up to you to decide which roles you're most comfortable with and which may not be for you.*

- *As you travel along this journey, be open to trying out as many roles as possible. You may find that some roles you never even thought about are just right for you!*

Next, let the girls know that on this journey, they have the chance to earn three important leadership awards: Reach Out! Speak Out! and Try Out! You might say:

- *What you do to earn these three leadership awards will give you a chance to see all the roles available to women and girls—roles that you might want to try, too.*

- *These awards also give you the chance to change the world—right here in your own community!*

Let the girls know that the Award Tracker in their book (pages 76–78) gives them a place to check off all the steps they accomplish toward their awards. Let them know that they'll do some steps together along the journey and some they'll enjoy on their own. Then say:

- *These journey awards are the most important awards in Girl Scouting before the Bronze, Silver, and Gold awards, which are our highest awards.*

- *In fact, the awards you earn on this journey, or any Junior journey, are required before you start on a Bronze Award Project. As you earn these journey awards, you'll gain the valuable leadership skills needed to plan and carry out a project. Those are the same skills you need to follow through on for a Bronze Award Project—and they are skills you'll find useful no matter what you do in life.*

- *And you'll have fun earning the awards because you'll develop more confidence, meet new people, and join with your sister Juniors to make a difference.*

Artists' Presentations

If artists were invited to this gathering, ask the girls to visit the various "stations," so they can mingle with the artists, take in the art, and experiment with some of the art mediums.

Take the Stage

Get the girls moving with this role-play game about "active" roles for girls and women. Invite the Juniors, one at a time, to choose one of the slips of paper on which you wrote the active roles listed below. After each girl chooses a role, ask her to jump into the "spotlight" and act out the role quickly, in just 5 to 10 seconds, as the other girls try to guess what role she's playing. When her time is up, have the girl say who guessed her role correctly or call out what her role was. Then another girl takes the stage. Continue the game until all the girls have had two or more turns at playing a role.

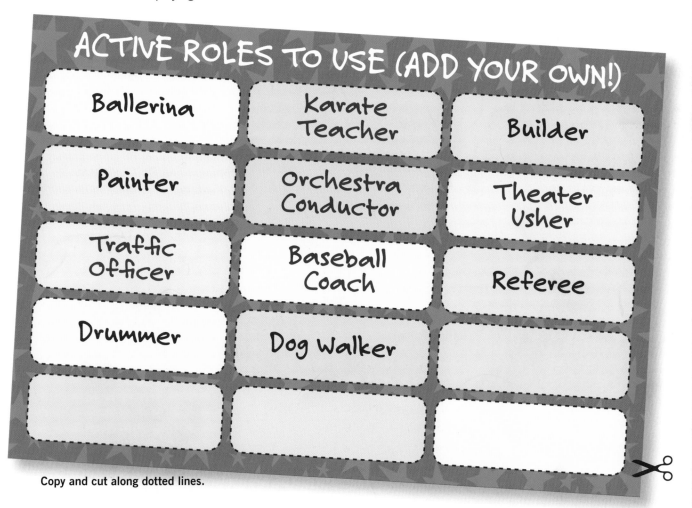

ACTIVE ROLES TO USE (ADD YOUR OWN!)

Ballerina	Karate Teacher	Builder
Painter	Orchestra Conductor	Theater Usher
Traffic Officer	Baseball Coach	Referee
Drummer	Dog Walker	

Copy and cut along dotted lines.

HOW TO DECORATE THE PROP BOX?

Let the girls know that their box doesn't have to be "perfect." What's important is that they experiment with the materials and have fun collaborating. Explain that they can "mix it up" and change their minds as they go.

You might suggest that the girls use theater and film motifs, such as images of a stage curtain, spotlights, costumes, movie screens, ticket stubs.

If the girls want to be able to carry the box easily, suggest that they poke holes in its sides and pull fabric or yarn through the holes to create carrier handles.

WHAT TO PUT IN THE PROP BOX?

Most anything will do: flashlights, binoculars, candles, hats, scarves, paintbrushes, spatulas, mirrors, aprons, galoshes, umbrellas, sunglasses, gardening tools, a jump rope, books, swimming goggles, bike helmet, briefcase, medical bag, sports team jacket.

Inside the Prop Box

Introduce the activity by letting the girls know that theater companies keep prop boxes backstage to hold all the props they use in their productions. Say something like:

- *A prop can be anything an actor needs to perform her role, such as a book, flowers in a vase, or a phone. Prop is short for property.*

- *Let's make a Team Prop Box that you can use to store props, big or small, along this journey.*

- *The Team Prop Box can hold objects that remind you of all the roles you play or want to play. You might put a friendship bracelet in the box to show your role as a friend, a Girl Scout pin or book to represent that you're a Girl Scout Junior, a wooden spoon to represent that you're a chef, or a compass to show that you're a camper. You can add to this prop box all along the journey, and you'll dip into it from time to time to try on new roles, too.*

Then bring out a large box (or another container of your choice) and the available art supplies and invite the girls to team up to decorate their Team Prop Box as they like.

Customize the Journey

Take time now to ask the girls as a group how they might like to make the journey their own. You might ask:

- *Would you like to celebrate earning the awards with small ceremonies along the way or one big one at the end?*

- *Are you interested in planning trips to a storytelling festival or an art museum, or to taking in a performance of a children's theater production or a concert?*

- *Are you up for an outdoor adventure with stories around the campfire?*

- *Would you like to tell a story in crafts by making individual prop boxes, a team scrapbook, or other projects?*

Keep these ideas in mind and add to them as you and the girls explore the journey's themes.

aMUSE-ing Snacks

SANDWICH "ROLE"-UPS

WHAT YOU NEED:

- lavash bread, flour tortillas, or whole loaves of bread with the crusts removed and the bread sliced horizontally.

- yogurt cheese or hummus, shredded carrots, shredded zucchini, turkey, or roasted red peppers, and shredded lettuce or an interesting leafy green such as arugula.

Invite the girls to enjoy a fun snack of "role"-ups—sandwiches rolled with assorted fillings.

DIRECTIONS

Spread yogurt cheese or hummus on the bread or tortillas, top with desired fillings (see list at left), roll up tightly, and cover with plastic wrap. Slice the rolls like a jelly roll when ready to serve. You and your Network can prepare the "role"-ups in advance, or each girl can play the role of chef and assemble her own.

Closing Ceremony: Roles and More Roles!

Gather the girls in a circle and ask them to take turns naming one of the many roles they already have in life and one new role they'd like to try. Then have the girls end with a friendship squeeze.

Looking Ahead to Session 2

Before the Juniors head out, ask them to be on the lookout for all of the roles they see girls and women take on all around them—those who help them out, teach them, give them rides, listen to them, and inspire them. You might say: *We'll share some of the roles we've seen next time we get together and get started on earning the first award in the journey. So, be sure to bring your books with you.*

Also let the girls know that next time, they'll make a fun snack together (see page 39, but don't spoil the surprise by saying too much!), and ask whether they prefer to make it using pesto or tomato sauce, a puree made from berries or mango, or another colorful sauce they all like. (Remember that some pesto sauces contain nuts, so check for allergies before offering it as a choice.) Reach out to your Network for the desired snack ingredients, including rice crackers.

Also contact your Network to gather a range of props to start off the Juniors' Team Prop Box. You'll want enough items so all the girls have several to choose from for the next session's closing ceremony (see suggestions on previous page).

NEW ROLES, NEW FOODS

The *aMUSE*-ing snacks along the journey may be new to the girls. So point out to them that just as it's fun to try new roles, it's can also be fun to try interesting new foods. Who knows? They may even find a favorite new fruit or vegetable—and a novel way to enjoy it!

Confidence grows as girls think about inspiring role models in their lives!

Girls Can Be Anything!

AT A GLANCE

MAKE THE MOST OF THE GIRLS' BOOK

The activities and discussions in this session correspond to "All About Roles," starting on page 10 in the girls' book.

Goal: The Juniors continue to explore the many roles available to them and start to learn about stereotypes.

- Opening Ceremony: Girls Are Supposed to Be . . .

- Time to Mingle

- Logs and Leaders

- Quick Draw

- *aMUSE*-ing Snacks: Quick-Draw, Open-Face Sandwiches

- Role-Play Switcheroo

- Closing Ceremony: A New Role to Try

MATERIALS

- **Logs and Leaders**: girls' books and pens or pencils

- **Quick Draw**: drawing paper, pencils with erasers

- ***aMUSE*-ing Snacks**: see page 39

- **Role-Play Switcheroo**: sticky notes, each with a large red or blue dot, one of each for each girl

- **Closing Ceremony**: Team Prop Box with new props collected from Friends and Family Network

PREPARE AHEAD

- Put a red or blue dot on each sticky note, creating enough notes so all the girls can have one of each color.

- Place snack sauces in bowls or squeeze bottles for the "Quick Draw" snack.

- Place the props from your Network into the Team Prop Box for the Closing Ceremony.

Opening Ceremony: Girls Are Supposed to Be . . .

Have the girls sit in a circle and ask them to take turns naming one thing that they think girls are expected to be in life. Let the girls come up with their own expectations; don't put any ideas in their heads. They might say sweet, always nice, good students, or helpful, or they might say athletic, artistic, or neat. Or they may say something entirely different.

After each girl has named one expectation, say something like:

- *There's nothing wrong with being any one of these things, if that's what you truly are. In fact, sometimes it's good to meet expectations, like getting passing grades in school and having good manners.*

- *But you don't need to meet an expectation that isn't good or really doesn't feel right to you.*

- *You don't want to be a certain way just because someone else thinks you should. Don't ever feel any pressure to be something you're not. For example, if you don't see yourself as a girly-girl, you wouldn't want to put on a dress with bows and ruffles. That just may not feel like you! And, hey, the opposite is also true: Frill it up when it suits you!*

Invite the girls to stand up and give a good shake, to shake off anything they don't believe they have to be. Then ask each girl to say one thing that helps describe who she really is. After each one speaks, invite the group to say, *That's who you're supposed to be!*

BE CLEAR ABOUT EXPECTATIONS

Make sure the girls understand the difference between good and useful expectations, like earning passing grades in school and being respectful, and expectations that are unrealistic or not true for them, such as being a star athlete when they'd rather be painting landscapes. That difference is what this Opening Ceremony is all about.

OPTION: MINGLING AMONG FRIENDS

If the girls in the group already know each other, try this variation: After the leader shouts "Freeze," the girl who gets pointed to calls out the name of the girl opposite her in the circle, and names one thing she knows about her.

Time to Mingle

Keep the girls active with this version of the vocal warm-ups that actors do to loosen up before they rehearse or perform. Here, the girls learn more about one another and their roles in daily life. You might say something like:

What we are about to do might seem really silly, but it's something actors like to do to loosen up before a performance.

Ask for a girl to volunteer to be the leader, and then get them playing the game by offering these directions:

- *Start by walking in a circle, and mumbling "mingle, mingle, mingle . . . ," as you go. Try to face one another as you walk so you're not just looking at your feet or the back of the girl in front of you.*

- *Keep walking and mumbling "mingle" until the leader shouts, "Freeze!"*

- *When "Freeze" is called, stop and face the girl opposite you across the circle. Then the leader points to one of you. If the leader points to you, call out your name and one thing about yourself: "My name is _____" and _____ ("I love dogs," "I play guitar," "I'm building a robot").*

- *Then the leader points to the girl across the circle. She repeats what the first girl said, but in a tone the leader decides, such as "happily," "very tired," "rushed," "boldly," "like you are very curious," "whiny," "like you have a cold," "angrily," "giggly, like a little kid," "formally, like a president," and so forth.*

- *Then another girl will volunteer to lead the group, and you'll all start again walking and mumbling, "Mingle, mingle." We'll wrap up when you've all had a chance to be the leader and everyone has had a chance to speak.*

Then you might ask the girls what they noticed about trying on different roles and attitudes by changing their tone of voice. Try some questions like these:

- *What roles and voices did you like? Which were your favorites?*

- *Which didn't you feel comfortable with? Why?*

Logs and Leaders

Ask the girls to turn to the Casting Call Log on page 16 of their book, and let them know that filling it out is a step toward their Reach Out! Award. Explain that the log is a place to list all the women they meet in their daily lives and the roles they play. Say something like:

Page 16–17, girls' book

- *At the end of our last session, I asked you to be on the lookout for all the roles girls and women play in your life. Think about the past few days and all the women you saw—at home, on the way to school, in the halls, in class, at lunch, after school.*

- *In your Casting Call Log, write down who you saw and the roles they were playing.*

- *If you don't know their names, write their roles. If there are just too many, write a few for now. You can fill in the rest later.*

Take a few moments for the girls to share their lists with one another. Then get a discussion going with questions like:

team talk!

- *How many roles are you seeing the women in your life play?*

- *Which of these women play more than one role? What are they?*

- *Which of these women do you consider leaders, either in their own lives or in the community? Why?*

- *What leadership traits do you see in them that you also see in yourself?*

- *Which leadership traits do you see in them that you aspire to?*

- *Now, think about the Girl Scout Law and all the values in it. Which of those values do these women seem to honor in the roles they play?*

- *Which of these values do you also honor?*

- *Which roles played by these women might you like to try?*

Congratulate the girls on getting started with their logs and taking a step toward earning their Reach Out! Award. Encourage them to keep filling out their logs as they see more women and girls in their daily lives, and let them know they'll share the logs again when they get together next time.

KEEP DISCUSSIONS FREE FLOWING

These and other suggested discussion questions are just that: suggestions. Feel free to omit some or add in others of your own, and let the conversations go where the girls take them.

And if you need to get the discussion about women and their roles going, offer a few roles that you have noticed. Example: the woman who delivers my mail, the veterinarian who cares for my cat.

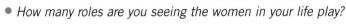

Quick Draw

Hand out drawing paper, pencils, and erasers and let the girls know they are about to try a fun way to find out how they picture various roles in life. You might say, *I am going to call out roles and you have one minute to draw the first picture that comes to mind.* Let them know that just a quick sketch is needed—even a stick figure is fine!

Possible roles: tennis player, newscaster, farmer, model, dentist, dancer, mayor, doctor, nurse, grocer, waiter, flight attendant, pilot, golfer, basketball player, firefighter, police officer, president, skier, bike racer, mail carrier, banker, pet shop owner, veterinarian, gym teacher, science teacher, librarian, secretary, math teacher, English teacher, college student, scientist, scuba diver.

Now get the girls talking about who they see on TV or in the movies in those roles, whether they are mostly males or females, and how what they see may have affected the way they think about certain roles. You might ask:

- *Why do you think you drew that role as a woman (or man)?*

- *Do you know someone who plays that role in real life? Or do you see someone on TV or in the movies who plays that role? Do you ever base your ideas of what someone in a role is like by what you see on TV or in movies without meaning to?*

- *Could someone older (or younger) play that role, too?*

QUICK DRAW, PART 2: QUICK-CHANGE ARTIST!

Call out one of the characteristics listed below and ask the girls to erase and change one of their drawings to be the opposite of what it now is. Point out that these attributes are some of the ones that people might unthinkingly use to limit a person's roles, and that being one way or the other shouldn't stop people from trying out roles. For example, if the girls drew a male dentist and you call out "gender," they erase and change the dentist's hair and face to be female because both women and men can be dentists. Do as many rounds of "Quick-Change Artist!" as the girls like, using these prompts:

- Gender (male/female)

- Age (young/old)

- Size (short/tall; large/small)

STEREOTYPES = LIMITED ROLES

To help the girls understand what stereotypes are, you might say something like:

Think about how, in our own minds, we sometimes limit the roles that people in the world can play.

For example, you might not think of your dad as someone who would braid your hair or help you pick out a party dress. Or you might think that a boy who's really good at science wouldn't also be good at baseball.

When we limit the roles people can play—even just in our minds—we put people in a role we choose for them, rather than a role they choose for themselves. That's what we call stereotyping!

As they discuss stereotypes, add in even more examples that you are aware of—and encourage the girls to do the same!

aMUSE-ing Snacks

QUICK-DRAW, OPEN-FACE SANDWICHES

Invite the girls to have some fun "drawing" creatively (with the pesto or fruit or vegetable purees or sauces—whatever the girls decided) on whole-grain rice cakes or bread. The sauces can be applied with small kitchen brushes or they can be placed in squeeze bottles, with which the girls can easily "draw." What the girls choose to "draw" is up to them!

Role-Play Switcheroo

Without realizing it, the Juniors may be playing out stereotypical gender roles in their daily lives. To make the girls more conscious of stereotypes, invite them to take turns role-playing girls and boys in a classroom situation. The roles to play: one teacher and an even number of girl and boy students.

Let the girls choose whether they want to be "girl" students and wear sticky notes with blue dots, or "boy" students and wear red dots. Encourage them to divide into equal numbers of "girls" and "boys." Ask for a volunteer who will play the teacher, who might be male or female, and for suggestions from the Juniors on the topic of the day's lesson—something in math, science, language arts, or current events, for example—which should be something they've studied in school and know fairly well.

Invite the girls to act out a typical class scenario, with the "teacher" standing in front, asking questions and encouraging discussion. Halfway through the role-play, ask "girls" and "boys" to switch stickies and roles. After the role-play, encourage the girls to discuss what happened. You can guide the discussion with such questions as:

- *Who put their hands up the most, "boys" or "girls"?*
- *Who offered their opinions the most?*
- *Who disrupted most, "boys" or "girls"?*
- *How did being a "boy" or a "girl" make you feel or act differently?*
- *Is there anything you now want to change about how you act in class? If yes, what? Why?*

Drawing on the information provided in the "Stereotypes=Limited Roles" sidebar on page 38, ask girls to consider whether they think they ever limit the roles they can play in their own lives. How about the roles of others around them? Let them know that they may do this without even thinking. Here are some conversation ideas:

CRAFT-Y OPTION: REMINDERS TO WEAR OR USE

If the Juniors love to make crafts, maybe they'd enjoy making something—a bracelet, a pocket card, or a bookmark—that serves as a reminder about avoiding stereotypes.

- *When we think about people in only one way, it's an easy shortcut for our brains—but it's not necessarily the right thing to do!*

- *After all, you wouldn't want others to think about you in only one way, would you? That might limit the roles you could play and the ways you could be in the world. That wouldn't tell your whole story!*

- *Think about how, in our minds, we sometimes limit the roles people can play in the world. For example, you might not think of your dad as someone who would help you choose a party dress. Or you might not think that your mom would be the one to teach you to throw a baseball.*

- *When we limit what people can do—even just in our minds—we put them in a very limiting role. They might rather play a different role, or a whole range of roles. It's best that they choose their own roles! When we choose narrow roles for people based on just one attribute, like being a boy or being a girl, that's what we call stereotyping!*

- *Have you ever heard the word "stereotype" before? How have you heard it used? Certainly people can stereotype based on the ways they think girls and boys should be, but they can also stereotype based on other things, like a person's height or heritage. When and in what ways have you noticed people stereotyping others?*

Wrap up the discussion by pointing the girls to the "Stereotype Tracker" on page 27 in their book. Encourage them to use it to write down the stereotypes they notice in their daily lives—at home, at school, at their place of worship, anywhere they might see them in their community. Get them started by saying: *What's a stereotype you just noticed about being in the classroom, and what can you do about it? Write that in your tracker right now.* Then encourage the girls to keep filling out the tracker on their own, and let them know it will help them zero in on a stereotype they care about for their Speak Out! Project.

OPTION: MORE GENDER SCENARIOS TO TRY

If the Juniors enjoy the Role-Play Switcheroo, offer one or more of these other boy-girl scenarios. Let the girls know there is no right or wrong way to be—they're just acting out what they've seen in their own lives.

Scenario 1

An election for officers—president, vice-president, secretary, treasurer—for school or after-school groups. (Who gets nominated for which roles? Who gets elected? Who speaks up for whom? Who votes for whom?)

Scenario 2

Recess or playtime in a schoolyard, playground, gym, or park. (Who uses the basketball court? Who stands around and talks? Who gets invited to play games? Who plays to win?)

Scenario 3

Preparations for a science fair where refreshments are served. (Who sets up the tables? Who prepares the food? Who chooses and puts up the decorations? Whose exhibits get the most attention?)

 **Closing Ceremony: A New Role to Try**

Gather the girls in a circle around the Team Prop Box, and invite them to take turns choosing a prop that looks interesting to them. Ask them to name a role they might use it in, and say if it's a role they already play or one they might be interested in trying out.

Looking Ahead to Session 3

Ask the girls to bring in a new prop for their Team Prop Box that signifies one of their roles in life.

Reach out to your Network for photos of women and girls in a variety of real-life roles for "I Wonder . . ." (page 43) and for snack foods (see page 47).

Pages 54–55, girls' book

Girls learn more when they interview local women about their many real-life roles.

CALLBACKS

SAMPLE SESSION 3
Callbacks

MAKE THE MOST OF THE GIRLS' BOOK

The activities and discussions in this session correspond to "All About Roles" and "The Callback," pages 10–23 and 28–35 in the girls' book.

Pages 14–15, girls' book

Pages 28–29, girls' book

AT A GLANCE

Goal: The Juniors reach out to women in their community to explore all the roles available to them.

- Opening Ceremony: I Can, I Am

- Casting Call Check-in and "I Wonder . . ."

- Reaching Out: Planning the Team "Callback"

- *aMUSE*-ing Snacks: Green Goddess Dip and Veggies

- Closing Ceremony: Admire, Inspire

MATERIALS

- **Opening Ceremony:** Team Prop Box and props brought in by the girls

- **Casting Call Check-in and "I Wonder . . .":** photos of women in real-life roles

- **Reaching Out:** copies of planning sheet and invitations

- *aMUSE*-ing Snacks: see Green Goddess Dip and Veggies recipe in girls' book, page 55

PREPARE AHEAD
- Read "Keep a Casting Call Log" and "The Callback" in the girls' book, pages 16–17 and 28–35.

Opening Ceremony: I Can, I Am

Gather the girls in a circle and ask them to take turns sharing their new props with the group. Each girl might introduce her prop and name the role it represents as she places it in the Team Prop Box. The girls might also share why they chose the prop and how they envision themselves using it.

Casting Call Check-in and "I Wonder . . . "

Check in on how the girls are doing in filling out their Casting Call Logs. You might ask: *What has surprised you most about the roles of the women and girls you find all around you?*

Then gather the girls around the various photos you've collected that show girls and women in real-life roles. Invite the Juniors to choose one or more images they like and are curious about. Suggest that they take turns completing this sentence: I wonder what it's like to be a _____ (singer, teacher, pilot, judge, scientist, swimmer, clothing designer, etc.), and then coming up with a question to ask the girl or woman: I would ask her: _____?

If more than one girl picks the same photo, encourage each girl to come up with a different question.

team talk! Reaching Out: Planning the Team "Callback"

For the second step in earning their Reach Out! Award, the girls are asked to do a Callback or interview with one woman from their Casting Call Log. The "Talk About Roles" section of their book (pages 28–31), steps through a series of questions to ask the woman during the Callback. If the girls prefer to tackle this award step as a team, they can host a panel discussion (at a future gathering or at another designated time).

THE CALLBACK: TEAM OR SOLO EFFORT? GIRLS' CHOICE!

Doing a Callback (an interview) with a woman or older girl to learn about her roles lets the girls explore the range of roles available to them. If they team up for a panel discussion, they'll get to meet even more women and see that even more roles are open to them!

Of course, the Juniors might conduct an interview with a woman from their logs on their own, or pair up for interviews, taking turns asking questions and writing answers.

In either case, have the girls' parents or guardians approve the interview choice and go along for the interview. Beforehand, guide the girls through the suggested interview questions on page 29 of their book and give them the chance to write their own questions.

LET THE GIRLS DO THE PLANNING!

Making decisions about questions to ask, roles to play, and other details is a great way for the girls to learn to scope and scale a plan for themselves.

By planning the panel discussion, they'll see how formulating a plan can help foster teamwork, create enthusiasm, and build momentum to reach an objective. They'll use these skills as they plan and carry out their Bronze Award projects and any projects in life.

Maybe you and the girls can think of examples in their lives right now when planning comes in handy!

KEEPING THE DISCUSSION GOING

Remember, the goal for the panel is to help the Juniors engage with a few women about their roles. The girls might be interested in keeping the discussion going beyond earning their award.

You can always make more opportunities for them to meet women by inviting a female firefighter, engineer, architect, veterinarian, referee, doorman (or doorperson) to gatherings to broaden their ideas about roles for women.

If this team option interests them, explain that a panel discussion is a group of people who come together to talk about a topic in front of an audience. Say something like:

- *Most panel discussions are led by a "moderator," who keeps the conversation flowing by asking questions of the panelists as a group or individually.*

- *The audience also has a chance to ask questions. So a panel discussion is a great way to learn about a particular topic and share ideas.*

- *We can hold a panel discussion to learn more about the roles played by the women in your Casting Call Logs. After the women talk about the roles they play, we'll have a chance to ask them questions. Let's use the questions on page 29 of your book to think about what we want to ask.*

- *But, first, let's decide who we want to invite to be on our panel. Let's think about which women on your Casting Call Logs you'd like to get to know better, and which roles interest you the most and why.*

Depending on the size of the group, it might not be possible for each girl to invite a woman for the panel. So you might suggest that they limit the size of the panel. Or they might limit its scope—by inviting only artists, for example. Or each girl might nominate a woman for the panel and then all the women's names are put in a hat and a set number of names are chosen, just like a raffle. Say: *We'll ask these women first. If they can't come, we'll go back and pull out more names until we have a full panel.*

Once the girls have a group of women to invite to their panel discussion, distribute copies of "Planning Our Panel Discussion" (opposite page and page 46) and go over this planning sheet as a group. Walk the girls through the questions on page 29 of their book, too. They might use some of those questions and also come up with some of their own to ask their panelists.

When the girls are set on how the panel will play out, have them decide on the various roles they will play during the panel discussion. Distribute copies of the invitation template, page 46, to those girls who will create any needed invitations. Of course, the girls can come up with their own invitations, too. The template may give them ideas.

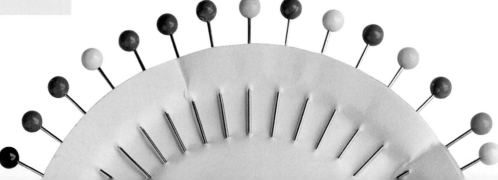

Planning Our Panel Discussion

1. The When, Where, and Who:

When . . . .

Where . . . .

Who's invited . . . .

. . . .

. . . .

. . . .

Call, e-mail, or talk in person with the panelists to confirm their attendance.

2. The Questions We'll Ask (see page 29 in your book for ideas):

. . . .

. . . .

. . . .

. . . .

3. The Roles We'll Play:

- Who will greet the panelists and show them where to sit?

- What Opening Ceremony will we have? How will we include our guest panelists?

- Who will be the moderator for the panel discussion?

- In what order will we ask our panelists to speak? For how long will they speak? What topics do we want to ask them to speak about?

- Who will keep time and let each panelist know when her time is up, so that each panelist gets equal time to speak?

- After all the panelists speak, who will ask the various questions we've come up with and in what order? Will we have one moderator or will all girls take a turn asking a question?

- Who will wrap up the discussion and thank the panelists for attending?

4. Who will set up the room where the discussion will be held? (Be sure that the panelists sit facing the Juniors and any other audience members.)

5. Will we serve refreshments? If so, who will take charge of that?

6. Who will be the "clean-up crew"?

Invitation template:

We'd Like You to Join Our Panel Discussion!

You've been chosen by our Girl Scout Junior group

to take part in a panel discussion about the many roles women play in the world. We'd like you to join a small group of women

on [date/time] .... at [location] ....

to talk about the roles you play and why you play those roles.

Your participation means so much to us! You will be helping us earn an important award on the leadership journey *aMUSE!*, which is about exploring all the roles available in the world to women and girls.

Please let us know if you can join us by [calling or e-mailing]

[provide a way to contact the Junior group's adult volunteer].

We look forward to talking with you.

aMUSE-ing Snacks: Green Goddess Dip and Veggies

When the Juniors are ready to enjoy the dip and veggies based on the recipe in the girls' book, let them know that this snack is in honor of the muses featured throughout the journey. Before the girls dig in, get them thinking and talking by saying something like:

- *Have you met the muses in your book yet? You know the word "amuse" is about fun and entertainment, but what about the word "muse" hidden inside it?*

- *In ancient times, muses were believed to be goddesses who inspired creative people. Today a muse is anyone, real or imaginary, who helps you imagine and create.*

- *Who's your muse? Maybe it's one of the women or girls in your Casting Call Log, or one of the panelists!*

Closing Ceremony: Admire, Inspire

Ask the girls to close their eyes and envision a role that they admire or that inspires them. Ask them to think about how that role makes them feel. Then let them know that actors use "body language" to express a feeling. Give this example: *To show what feeling proud looks like, you'd smile, push up your chin, and pull your shoulders back.* Ask the girls to keep their eyes closed and use body language to show the feelings the role inspired in them. Close by saying: *I admire all of you for trying on new roles!*

Looking Ahead to Session 4

Check in with all invited panelists to be sure they can attend and know the correct date, time, and place of the discussion. Reach out to your Network, too, in case you need a backup panelist or two.

If the Juniors are not hosting a panel discussion, start the session with a simple Opening Ceremony that makes use of the Team Prop Box, and then skip right to "Ads Assume . . . ." Ask the girls and your Network to bring in old magazines with ads for products aimed at children the girls' age, which they can tear or cut up for this activity. Aim to have extras on hand.

Also, ask your Network for volunteers to prepare the mini popcorn balls (see page 52 for recipe) for the next session's snack—with some Juniors, if possible!

EARNING THE REACH OUT! AWARD

Completing the Panel Discussion (or their own individual Callbacks) is the final step to earning the first award, Reach Out! The Juniors can earn the award right after the panel discussion. Take time during the planning for the girls to decide what ceremony they might like and who they want to invite to it.

BE A FAST NOTE TAKER!

Whether they're planning a panel discussion or doing the Callbacks on their own, the girls might find it fun to learn some note-taking tricks:

- To save time, use symbols and shorthand words. Use + for "and," @ for "at," w/ for "with," and w/o for "without," for example.

- Don't write down every word. Listen for the big ideas that really grab you.

- Collect more shorthand ideas from friends and family members.

Give the girls time to practice interviewing one another and using these shortcuts (they'll come in handy when txting!). And if they want a photo, remind them to take a camera along.

Confidence comes as girls reach out in their community to learn about women's roles.

TELL US YOUR STORY

Tell Us Your Story

MAKE THE MOST OF THE GIRLS' BOOK

The activities and discussions in this session correspond to "The Callback," page 28 in the girls' book. Reaching out to women in this simple way helps the Juniors widen the network of people they know in their community.

Pages 28–29, girls' book

AT A GLANCE

Goal: The Juniors learn more about the roles women play in real life and in the media.

- Opening Ceremony: Welcoming Our Guests
- The Panel Discussion
- Ads Assume . . .

- *aMUSE*-ing Snacks: Mini Popcorn Balls
- Reach Out! Award Ceremony and Closing

MATERIALS

- **Ads Assume . . . :** 10-20 ads and/or packaging for products marketed to children ages 9 to 12, such as toys, video or computer games, and sports clothes and equipment (make sure all the materials include photographs of children who are using the product); drawing paper, scissors, glue, and pens or markers

- **An *aMUSE*-ing Snack:** see page 52

- **Reach Out! Award Ceremony and Closing:** awards for each Junior

PREPARE AHEAD

- Make sure that the girls set up everything needed for the panel discussion and that all girls know the roles they'll play before, during, and after the discussion.

- If the girls are not hosting a panel discussion, bring out the Team Prop Box and organize any items you will use for a simple Opening Ceremony.

- Flip though any magazines the girls have brought in and you've collected for "Ads Assume . . . " and rip or cut out the ads you'll use.

- Set out the session's snack.

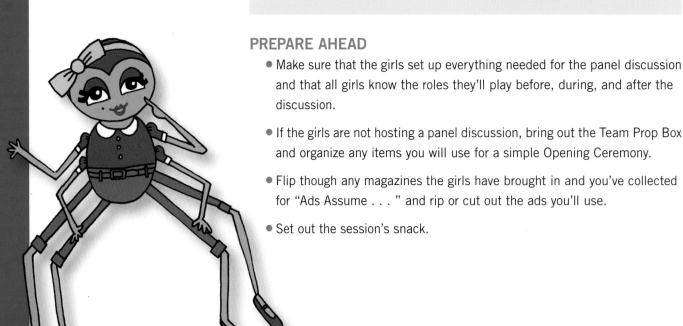

 Opening Ceremony: Welcoming Our Guests

Gather the Juniors in a circle around their guests and ask the girls to take turns stating their names and saying why they appreciate their visitors coming to their gathering today.

The Panel Discussion

Now's the time for the panel discussion to get under way according to the girls' plans. If no panel is planned, skip right to "Ads Assume . . . " (If there is no time afterward for the girls to enjoy "Ads Assume . . . ," save that activity for a future session.)

Ads Assume . . .

team talk!

Explain to the girls that advertising experts have the job of selecting pictures or photos to place in ads and on packaging for products the girls see every day, such as toys, games, and sports equipment. But it's usually a company's top executives who make the final decision about which image will sell their product best. Let the girls know that they will now play the role of those executives! Say something like:

How would you like to be an executive in charge of picking the pictures used to sell products to young people? You'll decide if the pictures are right for the ad or not.

Place the ads and packaging you and the girls have collected in the center of a table. Ask the girls to take turns choosing an item and placing it in one of three piles:

Products for girls

Products for boys

Products for girls and boys

Ask the girls to say quickly whether they agree with the choices for each pile and if not, explain why. (Let them know they do not need to agree on the choices, but they should listen respectfully to one another's views and feel comfortable speaking up to explain their own views.)

Before the "executives" decide whether to accept or change the images, pose
a few questions like these:

How would you describe the images you're seeing?

Who is shown using the product in these images?
Who's simply looking on?

Are you seeing any stereotypes in these images?

**How is it useful for advertisers to use stereotypical images
in their ads?**

When boys and girls are shown together, who is taller?
Who looks older?

Which images seem to appeal most to girls?
Which seem to appeal more to boys?

How does the image "make" you want to have the
product it's about?

Do any girls or boys you know use this product?
Do you know whether or not they like it?

Why might a boy or girl want or not want to use this product?

Now ask the girls to pile up any of the images (or packaging) they think need to be changed because they don't seem to represent a real view of the way girls or boys act in the world. Then, invite the Juniors to use the art supplies on hand to alter the ads (or packaging) so that they do represent a real view of the world as they know it. They might . . .

- paste or draw new images over the existing ones

- cut up the images and rearrange them in a way that they think makes better sense

- write what they want the people in the images to be saying by creating their own cartoon balloons and filling them in

- rewrite the ad or packaging copy

aMUSE-ing Snacks

MINI POPCORN BALLS

WHAT YOU NEED:

- 1 cup maple syrup

- 2 tablespoons butter

- 1 teaspoon vanilla extract

- ½ cup popcorn kernels (or 2-3 bags unflavored microwave popcorn), popped

- Optional mix-ins, such as mini chocolate chips, sweetened dried coconut, and nuts of your choice (allergies permitting)

Invite the girls and the panelists to enjoy this fun version of a traditional treat.

DIRECTIONS

Combine maple syrup and butter in a heavy saucepan over medium heat (cook to 260 degrees Fahrenheit on a candy thermometer).

Remove from heat, add vanilla, and stir it well. Pour over popcorn and mix with a big wooden spoon. Add in any optional mix-ins desired.

Shape into Ping-Pong–size balls carefully (mixture could still be a little hot!), and place on parchment paper until cool. Store in an airtight container until serving.

 Reach Out! Award Ceremony and Closing

Gather the Juniors together and ask each one to say one thing she learned while earning the Reach Out! Award. Then honor each girl with her award, and let them all know they can feel proud of having reached out into the community and found themselves a great group of muses—and maybe even some new friends. Encourage the panelists and any other guests to cheer and applaud.

Looking Ahead to Session 5

In the next session, the girls start to focus on creating their own story about stereotypes and the importance of not limiting the roles women and girls can play in life. They'll also decide whom to tell their story to, so they can inspire others to prevent stereotyping and keep a good change going!

Below is a handy list of the steps you'll guide the girls through toward their Speak Out! Award. On the next page is a Sample Planning Guide that shows you how a Speak Out! Project takes shape.

Keep in mind that during the next gathering, you'll want to guide the girls to set in motion a story-making and storytelling plan that gives them an opportunity to team up on a plan for change that they care about. If girls are really excited about their project, they may want to take their project even further!

Steps to the Speak Out! Award

1 As a team, the girls choose a stereotype they want to Take Action on. So, be ready to remind them that they've explored stereotypes in ads, in TV shows and movies, in their own life, and in their own thinking. They may have also heard about them from the women they met.

2 Together the Juniors create a story line about their chosen stereotype, and a clear call to action about how others can help bust that stereotype.

3 The girls decide on the best audience for their story. Who can help bust it and create lasting change?

4 The Juniors decide on a creative way to tell their story to their chosen audience so that it inspires others to help bust their stereotype. What muses will inspire the girls? Will their story take the form of a mural, a puppet show, a musical performance, a quilt … ?

Reach out to your Network for the ingredients for the S'mores snack, too. If your gathering place isn't equipped with a conventional oven and you aren't making the S'mores outdoors, a toaster oven will also be needed.

SAMPLE PLANNING GUIDE FOR A SPEAK OUT! PROJECT

STEREOTYPE	WHY BUST IT?	WHO IS YOUR BEST AUDIENCE?/WHERE WILL YOU PRESENT?/HOW WILL YOU REACH IT?	WHAT FORM MIGHT YOUR PROJECT TAKE?	WHAT CALL TO ACTION WILL YOU ASK OF YOUR AUDIENCE?
All girls are mean to each other	Girls are kind-hearted and funny, and help each other	Younger girls Invite Brownies to your meeting for a performance or reading, or perform for younger students at school Send an invitation to a Brownie group's adult volunteer. or get permission from teachers or school officials	Puppet show or picture book about a new girl and her friends who start a "mix-it-up" day where students sit at different tables at lunch	Switch tables and sit with someone you don't know at lunch every Monday, or start a "mix-it-up" lunch day at your school
Girls don't like math	Girls and boys like math	Parent-teacher groups Perform at a meeting of a parent-teacher group Contact the PTA to ask to perform at a meeting	Musical performance about an all-girls math Olympics team	Join together with a school, Girl Scout council, place of worship, or community center to organize and host a Math Day for girls
All firefighters are men	Women and men are firefighters	Girls our age, parent-teacher groups Host a reading and book signing event or a storytelling performance for other Juniors or at a PTA meeting Send an invitation to a Junior group's adult volunteer, contact the PTA	Graphic novel or storytelling presentation about a heroic female firefighter or an all-women fire company	Tell all the women in the audience to take time at least once a year to tell a girl about her work. Tell all the girls in your audience to take time each year to ask a woman about her work.

Creating stories about stereotypes gives girls confidence to bust them in real life!

A GATHERING OF STORYTELLERS

SAMPLE SESSION 5
A Gathering of Storytellers

MAKE THE MOST OF THE GIRLS' BOOK

The activities and discussions in this session correspond with the "Turning Acting into Action" (pages 36–43) and "Getting in on the Action" sections (pages 44–55) of the girls' book.

AT A GLANCE

Goal: The Juniors team up to create an educational and inspiring story about stereotypes that sends others a call to action—to stop stereotyping.

- Opening Ceremony: A Good Yarn
- First, the Stereotype
- Next, the Story Line

- Choosing Our Audience
- Deciding How to Tell Our Story
- Closing Ceremony: Celebrating Our Decisions

Pages 44–45, girls' book

MATERIALS

- **Opening Ceremony:** ball of yarn
- **First, the Stereotype:** chart paper, whiteboard or chalkboard, markers or chalk

- **Next, the Story Line:** paper, pens, or pencils
- **Closing Ceremony:** ingredients for S'mores and an oven, toaster oven, or campfire

Prepare Ahead

- In the girls' book, read "Storytelling with a Purpose," pages 38–39, and review the "Your Heart, Your Art, Your Part" and "Project Toolbox" activities, pages 44–47.

Opening Ceremony: A Good Yarn

Invite the girls into a circle. Hand the ball of yarn to one girl and ask her to begin a tale—or "yarn"—with one sentence. Her sentence can be as humorous or as outrageous as she likes. If she needs prompting, suggest: *"Once upon a time, _____ (character's name) sets out to _____ (do something or go somewhere)."* Once the first girl has spoken, she holds onto the thread end of the yarn, tosses the ball to another girl so the yarn unwinds, and calls out, "What happens next?" The second girl adds a silly or outrageous sentence to the story and then shouts, "What happens next?," and tosses the ball of yarn while still holding onto part of its thread, and so on around the circle.

When the story is finished, point out that the yarn has formed a web, connecting all the girls and symbolizing that the story they told belongs to them all.

Let the Juniors know that stories are central to what they'll be teaming up on for their Speak Out! Award. Say something like:

- *You and your sister Juniors will create a story about a stereotype that you care about, which will educate others about how it's wrong to limit the kinds of roles people have open to them.*

- *You'll tell this story to others to inspire them to stand up to stereotypes.*

- *Standing up to stereotypes is an important message, so you want your audience to hang on to your every word.*

- *In telling your story to an audience, you are being a leader. How? By educating and inspiring your audience about an issue you care about— stopping stereotypes!*

- *Maybe you've never thought of storytellers as leaders. But storytellers who tell stories with a message that help make the world better are leaders. They set change in motion when they speak out and offer their audience a call to action.*

- *As you tell your story and inspire others, you'll also get to try out even more new roles as a puppeteer, singer, muralist, dancer, musician, director, or writer—the choice is yours!*

HOW BIG A PROJECT?

As you guide the girls in creating their project, consider how much time you and they have, and how much support your Network can offer. A project doesn't have to be elaborate or polished. With even a modest effort, the girls will have a meaningful experience as long as they:

- Create a story to bust a stereotype they care about

- Tell their story to a live audience of any size

- Ask their audience to act to create lasting change

What's important is that their story has a focus, that it educates and inspires others, and that each girl plays a role in telling it!

NO LUCK WITH
STEREOTYPES?

If the Juniors aren't able to name any stereotypes and they also had trouble finding any as they looked around at school and throughout their daily life in order to fill out their Stereotype Tracker, take some time to talk with them about stereotypes they may have overlooked, especially in the media. You might mention these stereotypes:

- *All girls care about is makeup and clothes.*

- *Characters with glasses are smart.*

- *Cheerleaders and athletes are dumb.*

- *Boys are rough.*

- *Old people are "hard of hearing."*

Pages 26–27, girls' book

First, the Stereotype

Start by reminding the girls of all that they've learned about stereotypes so far. You might say:

- *A stereotype puts others into a group without thinking about them as individuals.*

- *One stereotype might be that all princesses do is wear gowns and jeweled crowns and wait around for their Prince Charming. Others might be that successful dancers have to be tall and skinny, or boys are better at science than girls, or girls care more about their looks than boys—those are all stereotypes.*

Then invite the girls to name any stereotypes they've noticed, especially since they've been asked to be on the lookout for them, in books, TV shows, movies, advertisements—or in real life. If none come to mind right away, remind the girls to refer to any stereotypes they listed in the Stereotype Tracker on page 27 of their book. Also encourage them to think about stereotypes they may have heard about from the women on their panel. Ask a volunteer to write each stereotype that gets named on chart paper or a whiteboard or chalkboard. Once everyone has had a chance to name a stereotype, get a discussion going. You might ask:

- *Which stereotype on our list limits you and other girls the most?*

- *Is there one stereotype that you hear a lot in our community? Why do you think that is?*

- *What can be done to stop that stereotype?*

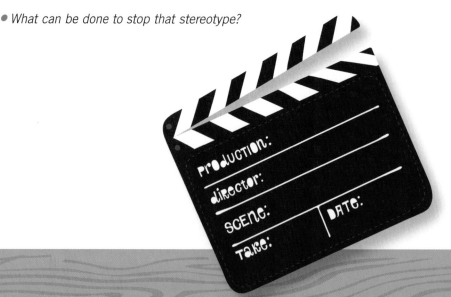

A STEREOTYPE TO TAKE ACTION ON!

Next, guide the girls to select a stereotype to focus their Speak Out! story on. You might ask:

- *Which stereotype that we've talked about today gets you most upset?*

- *Which of the stereotypes that really bother you would also be the most exciting to create a story about?*

- *What can be done to bust this stereotype?*

- *What would you put in your story to show how to bust this stereotype? Remember, you want your story to educate and start some lasting effort toward change.*

If the girls have trouble making a decision, you might ask them to narrow their list of choices to just two or three, and vote on a final choice. The aim is for the girls to come to a decision that they can all be comfortable with and accept.

AGREE TO DISAGREE!

Some girls may find it uncomfortable to disagree openly with others for fear of hurting someone's feelings. Encourage the girls to stand up for their own ideas, even when their sister Juniors might disagree with them. Hearing everyone's informed opinions is important; it can lead to new ideas and better decisions. Let the girls know that even when they don't all agree, they can still be great friends and accomplish great things together.

Next, the Story Line

Once the girls have picked a stereotype, encourage them to begin creating a story about it. Say something like:

- *Now we're going to create a story about the stereotype you chose as a group.*

- *Your story can be as realistic or fantastic, as funny or serious, as you want it to be.*

- *No matter what kind of story you create, its theme or big message is how busting stereotypes can benefit girls, women, and everyone!*

- *That way, the people you tell your story to will want to join you in busting the stereotype you care about!*

Start by reviewing together the tips for creating a story line on the next page of this guide. Then share some of these examples of stereotypes and story ideas. Let the girls know that they are just examples, and that they are making up their own story and characters based on the stereotype they chose to bust.

- If the stereotype is "All girls are mean to each other," their story can be about a girl who befriends the new girl at school and, together with her, starts a mix-it-up day at which everyone sits at different tables at lunchtime.

- If the stereotype is "Girls don't like math," their story can be about girls who form an all-girl math Olympics team and compete in the finals.

- If the stereotype is "All firefighters are men," their story can be about a girl who dreams of becoming a firefighter, becomes one, and ends up saving the day.

Then pass out paper and pencils, and get the girls talking and sharing ideas. Encourage them to keep going until they have a basic story line with a beginning, middle, and end that they all can agree on. Let them know that their story doesn't have to be perfect. They can change it as they move forward, perhaps even transforming it into a mural, puppet show, or other art form.

TIPS FOR CREATING A STORY LINE

The more ideas the better. Sometimes the best ideas don't come until the so-so ones are thought of first, so share whatever comes to mind, no matter how "out there." Take notes. Read them back now and then to spark more ideas.

- Figure out who the main character(s) will be:

- What is her name, age, and any other important information?

- What is she like? How does she act when things go well? When they go badly?

- When the story begins, show that something important is about to happen, or have something dramatic already happening.

- Figure out what happens next. A story shows how a character deals with the obstacles that get in her way.

- How does she go about busting the stereotype you (the group) chose?

- What or who gets in her way of reaching her goal? (The situation usually gets worse before it gets better.)

- What qualities does she rely on to overcome challenges?

Once the girls have come up with a story line they can all agree on, say something like:

- *Congratulations! You have an important story to tell and you've made great progress on it.*

- *Next, you will decide whom to tell your story to, and how to tell it. Will you want to tell it through dance, a mural, a puppet show, a graphic novel, a story quilt, or simply by reading or speaking it?*

- *It's up to you!*

CAPTURING AN AUDIENCE

Think about what the Juniors and their families do during the course of a week. What can the girls piggyback onto for telling their story—during school, after school, at regular weekend activities? Who do they see regularly who might be their audience?

Tap into a "ready-made" audience at a PTA meeting, another Girl Scout group's gathering, an after-school or other youth program, or events at a local library, school, or other public venue. Reach out to your Network and the Girl Scout community. Share with them what the girls are planning. They may be able to call or e-mail contacts to get things rolling.

Keep in mind that the girls' call to action for their audience can be simple and still effective. For example, if they create a mural to call attention to a stereotype they want to bust, they can simply ask anyone who views the mural to sign it as a commitment to join them in busting the stereotype, too!

Choosing Our Audience

Get the Juniors thinking and talking about whom they want to tell their story to, and what they want their audience to do or say once they've heard their story. Say something like:

- *The story you've created shows the unfairness of stereotyping and the courage it takes to challenge stereotyping.*

- *Who should hear your story? People who can help do something about it!*

- *For example, if your story is about girls at school who start a "mix-it-up" lunch day and sit with new friends in the cafeteria, who might do something like that? That's your audience— and that's what you want your audience to do once they've heard your story!*

- *Remember, you want your audience to join with you in busting stereotypes. That's making lasting change. That's what leaders do: They rally people to action!*

PROJECT COACHING TIPS

In both Sessions 6 and 7, check in with the girls to see . . .

- how their teamwork is going: Do they need any assistance in coming to an agreement on any aspects of their story? Are things going so well that they should huddle and give a cheer?

- if they're set with what they need to do—if anything— between sessions.

☐ Encourage a quick discussion about all parts of the project to be tackled ahead of and during the sessions. Ask: Is everyone's voice being heard? Does everyone have an active role?

☐ Reassure the girls that projects often require some trial and error, lots of idea sharing, lots of negotiating on diverse viewpoints, and a good dose of patience. Emphasize that when something isn't going well, it can be fun to fix it.

☐ Let them know the project doesn't have to be a perfect or professional work of art. What's important is that they tell their story in a way that inspires their audience to act.

☐ Encourage them to see that they are learning from what they are doing: They're building skills, trying new things, and growing as storytellers—plus changing the world!

Deciding How to Tell Our Story

Let the Junior team know that their strengths and interests as a group will come into play when they decide how to tell their story to their chosen audience. Refer them to "Your Heart, Your Art, Your Part" (pages 44–45 of their book), and say something like:

- *As you can see, there are lots of ways to have a role in telling a story.*

- *Think about the role you want to play. Think about what you love to do, and what you want to contribute to the group.*

- *Think about artists you've met on this journey. Whose work most appealed to you? Would you like to tell your story using their art form?*

- *It's good to consider whom you're telling your story to when you think about how you want to tell it to. For example, a younger audience might enjoy a puppet show or picture book that tells your story.*

Next, share these possible ways for the girls to tell their story to an audience:

- Onstage, with storytelling or a puppet show. Storytellers are like actors in a play, but they talk directly to the audience instead of addressing each other. Storytellers know the basic story, but they can change the words they use to tell it. They can use simple props and costumes, such as hats. In puppet shows, the storytellers use puppets to tell the story. Storytelling performances can be captured on video, with still photos, drawings, maps, or other elements added during editing.

- In pictures: with a mural, story quilt, story cloth, photos, or video. Murals are large paintings on the walls of buildings. The girls can use butcher paper to create their mural and display it indoors or outside. Story quilts are made up of separate squares that tell a story in sequence. Story cloths are one big panel with images that show parts of the story all at once.

- In song and movement, with a musical performance. Songs in any musical style can be paired with dance moves to tell a story.

- In words, with a picture book or graphic novel. Picture books are story books or illustrated books usually intended for young children who can't read yet or are learning to read. Graphic novels or comic books tell stories in pictures and words.

Guide the girls to make a team decision about how they will tell their story. Let them know they'll each have a role in creating the story in the art form they select.

Closing Ceremony: Celebrating Our Decisions

To celebrate all the big decisions made today on the girls' Speak Out! Project, make and enjoy the long-standing Girl Scout favorite, S'mores! Don't know how to make them indoors? Just look up Indoor S'mores on the Web. Or better yet, head outside and celebrate around a campfire!

Looking Ahead to Sessions 6–7

Sessions 6–7 are grouped together as time for the Juniors to get creative with their stereotype-busting story, so they can inspire their audience with it. The girls will use these two gatherings to transform their story into their chosen mode of creative expression, so remind them to bring any notes and ideas they've been jotting down. Now is a great time to invite back any of the artists from the kickoff, who can provide expertise and inspiration on the art form the girls have chosen. If possible, ask the artist about art materials and equipment to have on hand. Your local library will also have how-to books with detailed instructions to help you step the girls through creating stories in various mediums. Look ahead to the next sessions, and call on your Network to help gather any needed materials.

If the girls haven't yet enjoyed the "Ads Assume . . . " activity, make time for it in Session 6 or 7.

SAMPLE SESSIONS 6 & 7

Our Muse, Your Project

MAKE THE MOST OF THE GIRLS' PROJECT TIME

As the Juniors move forward on their project:

They could hang a quilt at the library, and the call to action could be that everyone who looks at it would be asked to sign a commitment to join the girls in their effort.

Keep in mind that the activities and discussions in this session correspond with "Turning Acting into Action" (pages 36–43) in the girls' book.

Pages 36–37, girls' book

AT A GLANCE

Goal: The Juniors turn their story into a form of creative expression that will educate and inspire others to stand up to stereotypes.

- Opening Ceremony: The Blob
- Time to Create!
- What's My Role?
- Bringing a Muse to Life

- *aMUSE*-ing Snacks: Musie Smoothies and "Break a Banana" Split
- Closing Ceremony: Crazy Curtain Calls

MATERIALS

- **Time to Create!:** whatever art supplies and other materials the girls need for their chosen project; computer if showing storytelling video; copies of the storyboard form (page 70)

- **What's My Role?:** copy of the Speak Out! Project Planner and

Sign-up Sheet; copies of the invitation

- **Bringing a Muse to Life:** any art supplies already on hand (if the girls will be doing this)

- *aMUSE*-ing Snacks: see page 74

PREPARE AHEAD

- Set out materials needed for the creative expression the Junior team has chosen.

- If you've invited a guest artist, talk with her about how she will assist the girls.

- Preview video of young people telling stories from the National Youth Storytelling Showcase Web site to share with the girls.

Opening Ceremony: The Blob

Let the girls know that actors sometimes use an exercise called "The Blob" to practice working well as a team. Explain to the girls that they will huddle together, shoulder to shoulder, facing any direction they like. The team becomes one creature, the Blob. Ask the girls to stand quietly, without speaking, and sense how the Blob wants to move. Then, invite everyone to move together, going with the movement, with no one actually leading. Ask: *Where will the Blob go? Let's see!*

Time to Create!

Gather the Juniors together around the materials they will use to tell their story, and let them know it's time to call on their creativity, energy, and teamwork to turn their stereotype-busting story into a work of art. Introduce the guest artist, if one has been invited, and let the girls know she's there to lend a hand and inspire their creative expression—to be a muse!

Whatever art form they're using, the Juniors can begin with a quick review of their story. Ask them to pull out their story line and notes from their last gathering. Ask one girl to volunteer to recount how their story starts. Then ask the rest to take turns recapping the events as they happen in the story.

When they've finished, invite the guest artist to get the girls started. If there's no guest, share with the girls the appropriate descriptions and tips below, and use techniques and pointers from the how-to books you've found. (For the storyboard form, see page 70 in this book).

SECRETS OF STORYTELLING

Seeing and listening to other storytellers is a great way for Juniors to pick up some techniques. The Kids' Storytelling Club Web site offers excellent tips on storytelling. The girls might also enjoy watching videos of young people telling stories on the National Youth Storytelling Showcase Web site. As the girls view the videos, ask them to notice how the storytellers use the following techniques, and to think about how they can use them, too:

- gestures and facial expressions

- pauses before important words and emphasis on those words

- pauses for audience reaction

- different voices for different characters

MORE STORYTELLING SECRETS

Check your local library, too. Many children's librarians are experienced storytellers, and they might recommend resources for you and the Juniors. A storytelling festival, if there's one in your area, might make a great field trip.

MUSICAL PERFORMANCE

If the girls are telling their story as a song, they might want to do it hip-hop style, which is rhythmic, rhyming poetry recited rapidly to a beat. Once the girls write their lyrics, they can perform their story in any way they choose, perhaps by taking turns singing or reciting the lyrics as the others mime the actions.

PICTURE BOOK OR GRAPHIC NOVEL

Whether they're making a picture book or a graphic novel (a comic book), the girls might start by creating a sequence of scenes drawn with stick figures and rough shapes, using the storyboard form on page 70.

Next, have the girls, working individually or in pairs, sketch the illustrations, write the text, and design the pages. After a run-through with the whole group, invite the girls to color in all the pages, decide on a title, and create a title page with all their names or the name of their Junior group as author.

If the girls want more than one copy of their book, photocopy the pages, and then fasten, staple, or sew them together to make the finished copies.

STORYTELLING OR PUPPET SHOW

For their storytelling presentation, the girls will want to plan out what they will say in advance. Suggest that they start by thinking of their story as a series of scenes involving the various characters. They might want to take notes as they create their "script" or use an audio recorder as they talk it out.

Once the girls have planned out what they will say, get them to brainstorm ideas about props, costumes, and staging, such as whether they want to stand or sit as they tell their story. Let them know they'll have plenty of time to rehearse, and they can make changes to their "script" and other details as they go along.

MURAL.
STORY QUILT.
OR STORY CLOTH

For a simple mural, the girls might work together to create a storyboard (page 70), and then paint scenes from their story on butcher paper. Working from left to right, they might begin by sketching the images, in pencil or chalk, on a large piece of butcher paper or canvas. Once they're satisfied that the story fits, they might outline and fill in their work with markers and paint.

Story quilts can be easily fashioned from press-on fabric. A story quilt contains squares of fabric, each containing a single scene, sewn together in sequence to tell a story. Get the girls started by guiding them to work together creating a storyboard. Then have each girl, working with an image from the storyboard, use a fabric pen or marker to draw the image onto a square of fabric. Finally, make time for the girls to sew, glue, or iron the squares together, in order.

In a story cloth, events are shown as taking place all at once, rather than in sequence. Invite the girls to sketch out the story's characters and objects on a large piece of paper, to determine placement. Let the girls know that each one of them will be responsible for creating several images, which she might want to sketch to size on paper or fabric, cut out, then tape or glue to the large background cloth. The girls might also want to write a few words on the story cloth to explain the scene.

ANOTHER OPTION: STORY DANCE

Many ballets, such as "The Nutcracker" and "Swan Lake," modern dances, such as Twyla Tharp's "Movin' Out," and traditional Asian dances tell stories. Story dance blends acting and creative movement set to music and/or live singing to tell a story. If the girls have chosen to tell their story through dance, have them first work together to create a storyboard (page 70), and then translate their story into patterns of movement. One or more narrators might explain what's happening on stage.

Storyboard Template

Sketch out the characters and action in each scene, and add dialogue or details in the spaces below.

Speak Out! Project Planner and Sign-up Sheet

Who's our audience? ....

What's our call to action? ....

Where will we present our project? ....

When will we present it? ....

How will we invite our audience? ....

Who will we ask to help us? ....

What each Junior will do:

Name	Responsibility	Name	Responsibility

What other people will do to assist us:

Name	Responsibility	Name	Responsibility

What do we hope to accomplish with our Speak Out! Project? We'll make a difference because

. . . .

. . . .

Please attend our
Girl Scout Juniors' Speak Out! Presentation

Our Junior group .... has created a story to Speak Out! against a stereotype and the importance of not limiting the roles women and girls can play in life. You can help us bust a stereotype—and earn an important leadership award—by attending our presentation!

Date: ....

Time: ....

Place: ....

Please let us know if you can join us by ....

....
[provide a way to contact group's adult volunteer].

What's My Role?

Take some time to get the girls thinking about how they will present their story to their audience, and the roles they'd like to play when they present it. For example, if the girls have created a performance, they'll want to decide where and when to present it, and who will perform the roles onstage, backstage, and in the "front of the house." They'll also want to plan out how they will invite their audience, who will send the invitations (if using), how they will greet their audience on the day of the performance, and how they want to ask their audience to commit to their call to action.

Here are other ways the girls might present their story:

- For a picture book or graphic novel, they can hold an author event at a PTA meeting or Girl Scout gathering, where they read from their book, answer questions during a Q&A session, and sign copies.
- For a mural, quilt, or story cloth, they can hold a public unveiling at school during lunchtime or at a place of worship after the service, where they can talk about the work and how they created it.

Once the girls have decided how to present their story and what they'll need, pass around a planning and sign-up sheet, and ask each girl to write her name next to the role she chooses. Suggest that girls can take on more than one role, if they like.

Bringing a Muse to Life

Being creative isn't easy. That's why there are muses to keep the inspiration going! Though the Juniors are creating as a team, each girl might have her own muse (or several!). If time permits, each girl might use the art materials on hand to create a small picture or puppet of her muse (or muses), to remind her of what inspires her and how she inspires others, too. The girls might place their muses in the Team Prop Box as journey keepsakes.

LET THE GIRLS COACH THEMSELVES

You might want to share these questions that the girls can keep in mind as they rehearse:

1. Am I speaking loudly enough so the audience can hear me?

2. Am I speaking clearly enough so the audience can understand me?

3. Am I varying the way I speak so it sounds natural?

4. Am I using appropriate facial expressions and gestures?

aMUSE-ing Snacks

MUSIE SMOOTHIE

WHAT YOU NEED:

- 1½ cups fresh or frozen berries (strawberry, blueberry, raspberry, or a mixture)
- ½ cup low-fat plain yogurt (or rice milk, if there are dairy allergies)
- 1/4 cup orange juice
- 1 tablespoon honey
- ½ teaspoon vanilla extract

Invite the girls to make Musie Smoothies as a little salute to their muses and their creativity! The recipe below makes about 2 cups, so increase the amounts depending on the size of your group.

DIRECTIONS

Place all ingredients in a blender and blend until smooth. Enjoy!

"BREAK A BANANA" SPLIT

WHAT YOU NEED:

- bananas
- sorbet (or low-fat frozen yogurt)
- chocolate syrup
- whipped cream
- strawberries or chocolate sprinkles

Saying "Break a leg" is a way to wish a performer good luck before a performance. The girls might enjoy a "break a banana" snack, like a banana split, on one of their project creation days.

DIRECTIONS

For each banana split, slice a banana in half the long way. Place in a long, narrow dish or a bowl. Put small scoops of sorbet (or low-fat frozen yogurt) between the halves. Drizzle a little chocolate syrup and add a dollop of whipped cream. Add strawberries or chocolate sprinkles.

Closing Ceremony: Crazy Curtain Calls

A curtain call usually comes at the end of a performance. It's the traditional way for all the performers, and even the full crew, to take a bow as the audience applauds. Ask the Juniors to line up to take turns in a fun and crazy curtain call: One girl steps forward, turns to face the line of girls, and makes a playful curtain call by taking a bow and then being as silly as she likes. She might throw kisses to crowd, jump up and down, do a dance, or anything of her choice. Then the next girl steps forward to do her crazy curtain call, and so on, until all the Juniors have a had a turn.

Looking Ahead to Session 8

In the next session, the girls present their Speak Out! Project and earn their Speak Out! Award. So guide them to confirm the date, time, and location of their presentation, and to be sure that their chosen audience can make it. For a smooth presentation, you might want to add in some additional rehearsal time for the girls, ahead of the big day. Also call on your Network for any needed materials or snack ingredients.

SAMPLE SESSION 8
Showtime!

MAKE THE MOST OF THE GIRLS' BOOK

The activities and discussions in this session correspond to "Turning Acting into Action," pages 36–43 in the girls' book.

AT A GLANCE

Goal: The Juniors tell their story to educate and inspire others about the importance of stopping stereotypes.

- Opening Ceremony: Wacky Warm-up
- Showtime!
- Award Presentation and Closing: Earning the Speak Out! Award

MATERIALS

- **Showtime!:** whatever the girls need to present their story to their selected audience
- **Award Presentation and Closing:** Earning the Speak Out! Award: awards for each Junior

PREPARE AHEAD

- Make sure that the room is set up for the presentation, and that any needed equipment is in place and working.
- Check to be sure that the girls are ready to play their roles, and that they have everything they need to do so.

Opening Ceremony: Wacky Warm-up

The girls form a circle. A volunteer shouts out something silly ("wacky, wacky, wacky, woo," or "googly, googly, goo" perhaps) while repeating some movement, such as marching in place, or spinning in place, or touching toes). The girl next to her repeats what she says and does, and then adds a phrase and movement of her own. The next girl repeats both, adding her own phrase and movement. (As the phrases and moves pile up, let the later girls know it's OK to forget some of them!) Then invite the entire audience to repeat everything in unison.

◯ Showtime!

The girls present their story and then deliver their message to their audience, asking them to join with the Juniors to bust stereotypes and support women and girls in whatever roles they choose in life. (See examples in the final column of the Sample Planning Guide for a Speak Out! Project, on page 55.) The girls might ask the audience to make a pledge with them by completing these two sentences:

I was inspired by .... to .... I pledge to ....

Award Presentation and Closing Ceremony: Earning the Speak Out! Award

Have the girls present the Speak Out! Awards to one another by gathering together in a circle, so that each girl can first state why she enjoyed working on this project with the girl to her right, and then present an award to her. Let the girls know that the Speak Out! Award represents just what its name says: They have used their teamwork, creativity, and courage to speak out against stereotypes, and they've inspired others to speak out against them, too!

Looking Ahead to Session 9

Explain that the "last act" of the journey—to explore new roles and get started on earning their Try Out! Award—begins next session. Ask the girls to bring their books with their filled-in Role Call Logs to the next gathering. Let them know that they'll be creating self-portraits in whatever art medium they choose, from a doodle drawing to a sculpture made of twigs, bottle caps, and other found objects. Encourage them to collect and bring in found objects, if they wish.

Preview and select art history books, preferably ones that focus on art by women artists, to share with the girls during the "Defining Real Beauty" activity, on page 79. Also, reach out to your Network for the portraits of women and girls needed for the "Picture This" activity (page 81), and for small mirrors, one per girl, and a range of art supplies to use as the Juniors create their own self-portraits.

Now is a great time to invite back artists from the journey's kickoff, or any other artists, art students, or art teachers who can assist the girls with their self-portraits.

Girls gain confidence as they develop their own definitions of beauty.

Who I Am Now

MAKE THE MOST OF THE GIRLS' BOOK

The activities and discussions in this session correspond with "The Role of a Lifetime, Starring . . . YOU!" (pages 56–61) in the girls' book.

ACT 3, Scene 1:
The Role of a Lifetime,
Starring...YOU!

Pages 56–57, girls' book

AT A GLANCE

Goal: The Juniors explore what beauty means to them, how they see it themselves, and how it informs their story.

- Opening Ceremony: Me and You
- Defining Real Beauty
- Picture This!
- Mirror, Mirror
- Arty Party
- Closing Ceremony: This Is My Story! Where Will It Go?

MATERIALS

- **Defining Real Beauty:** art books offering a range of images; pad of sticky notes; chalkboard or whiteboard, or large sheet of paper; writing implements; range of art supplies (color pencils, paints, paper, construction paper, bits of fabric, foil, wrapping paper, buttons, found objects)

- **Picture This!:** A selection of portraits of women and girls in any medium (from books, magazines, or photos you have)

- **Mirror, Mirror:** hand mirrors, one per girl; variety of art materials, such as drawing paper, pens, markers, paint, clay, found materials, digital cameras

- **Arty Party:** each girl's finished self-portrait, tape, and whatever else the girls have decided on; ingredients for the "Arty Party Snack" (see page 83)

- **Closing Ceremony:** small slips of paper, pencils

PREPARE AHEAD

- If you've invited an artist, art student, or teacher, offer her a preview of the activities to determine how she can assist the girls.

- Set up the Arty Party space as needed, including ingredients for the "Arty Party Snack" (see page 83)

Opening Ceremony:
Me and You

Gather the girls in a circle. Ask one girl to start off by naming something she likes about herself and then asking the girl next to her, "What do you like about yourself?" If they're up for it, the girls can continue around the circle several times.

Defining Real Beauty

Remind the girls that they've just told a story to an audience about the importance of steering clear of stereotypes and not letting someone else's ideas limit what women and girls can do. Now it's time for them to explore their own thoughts and feelings about beauty and the importance of not getting "typed" into someone else's definition of beauty.

Invite each girl to leaf through the art books you've collected. Ask each girl to select one image that she thinks is beautiful based on her own ideas, and put a sticky note with her name on it on the image.

Once all the girls have chosen a work of art, get them going on a discussion of the art they chose—first in a general way and then by zeroing in on why each girl picked the image she selected, and all the various reasons the girls had for thinking of the art as beautiful. You might use some questions and conversation starters like these:

- *What do you notice about all the works of art that now have stickies on them?*

- *Are any of them alike in any way?*

- *How are they different?*

- *Now, let's all talk about why we chose the work of art we chose. Let's take turns showing our piece of art and explaining why we think it's beautiful. (Ask a girl to volunteer to make a list, as the girls speak, of all the reasons given for why the various works of art are considered beautiful. You might label this list "Qualities of Beauty.")*

Depending on the size of the group, the girls' answers may be quite varied. Guide them to see that "beauty is in the eye of the beholder"—one work of art may be beautiful to some girls and not beautiful at all to others.

chat time Next, ask the girls to look at the "Qualities of Beauty" list they've compiled. Ask them to take this list and, together, come up with a definition of beauty that they all agree on. Ask:

What does this definition say about beauty?

Now invite the girls to use the art supplies on hand to create their own image of beauty inspired both by the work of art they first chose from the art book *and* by their definition of beauty. Encourage them to create in any medium they like, whether 2-D or 3-D. Also suggest that they give a title to their creations. When the images of beauty are complete, they can arrange them in a "gallery" display for all to view and appreciate—and be further inspired by!

Picture This!

Get started by letting the girls know that portraits show more than what a person looks like on the outside. The best portraits might even reveal how someone thinks and feels, what she believes in, and how she sees her role in the world.

Then share the portraits of women and girls you've brought in to show the Juniors, and the self-portrait of Margaret Bourke-White on this page (other self-portraits by Bourke-White, and many portraits of her, can be found by searching her name on the Internet). Then get a discussion going with some questions like these:

- *How would you describe the woman (or girl) shown in each of these pictures?*
- *What's the first thing you notice about them?*
- *What's different about each of these women (or girls)?*
- *For example, what's different about their facial expressions? About their clothes, hair, and the way they hold their body?*
- *What questions would you ask these women (or girls)?*

Self-Portrait of an Artist
Margaret Bourke-White made many famous photographs over the course of her career, which included work for *Life* and *Fortune* magazines, time as a war correspondent, and chronicling the Great Depression. In this 1943 self-portrait, she stands next to the bomber from which she took combat photos during World War II.

Mirror, Mirror

Gather the girls around the hand mirrors and art materials. Invite them to play the role of artist, and create their own self-portraits. You might explain to them that before cameras became widespread, artists often used mirrors to study what they looked like, in order to create self-portraits. Suggest that the girls now look at their reflections in the mirror and consider these questions:

- What do you see?
- What don't you see that you want others to see you?
- What role do you want to play?

Then ask them to think about what pose, gesture, expression, clothing, and setting they want in their self-portraits. Let them know that they don't have to use what they see in the mirror if they choose not to. Maybe they prefer to depict themselves as they feel, not as how they look. Or perhaps they want to create an animal or object that symbolizes how they see themselves. Let them know that any or all of these options is fine.

Arty Party

Suggest that the girls turn the meeting space into an art gallery by taping their completed self-portraits to the walls or displaying them on tables around the room, and then hold an arty exhibit-opening party. The girls can have fun playing the roles of both artists and gallery visitors. They can walk around and view, compliment, and discuss each other's work, all while nibbling on an "Arty Party Snack" (see sidebar at right).

Closing Ceremony: This Is My Story! Where Will It Go?

Gather the girls in a circle and pass out the small slips of lined paper. Then say:

All along this journey you've seen how your story is changing and how you can add on new roles at any time.

If you had to write the title for your life story right now, what would that title be? Would you write, "Amelia, the Outdoor Adventurer" or 'Felicia, the Fantastic Cook" or "Lucy, the First Scientist to Live on Mars"?

Now, let's each take a few minutes and write down a title for our individual life story. Then we'll go around and share them.

Looking Ahead to Session 10

Ask the girls to try out the "Now, Head Out in a Hat or Scarf or . . ." activity in their book (page 69), which invites them to wear something a little different than what they usually wear, such as a cool hat or sunglasses, to see how it feels. Say to the girls: *For our next meeting, wear or bring in the accessory you tried out so we can enjoy a group fashion show!*

Also, let the girls know that they'll enjoy a Dance Party at their next session, too, so talk for a few minutes about what music the girls want to dance to. The girls and the Network might round up the music and any equipment needed to play it.

Reach out to the Network for ingredients for the Get-Up-and-Go Gorp snack and for photos of active women for "Our Bodies: Beautiful and Strong." You might ask the girls to bring in photos, too.

ARTY PARTY SNACK

Fruit and cheese are often served at art-gallery exhibit openings. The girls can go one better with arty kebabs. From a selection of bite-size fresh fruits and cheeses, the girls choose their favorites to thread on skewers, alternating fruit and cheese.

Girls supporting and appreciating their bodies—that's a confidence builder

Who I Might Be

MAKE THE MOST OF THE GIRLS' BOOK

The activities and discussions in this session correspond with "Inner Confidence, Outer Style" (page 62–75) in the girls' book.

AT A GLANCE

Goal: The Juniors explore how healthy bodies support them in taking on roles, and how they can support and appreciate their bodies.

- Opening Ceremony: Follow This Tune!
- Sharing Our Accessories
- Our Bodies: Beautiful and Strong
- OPTION: Dancing Hands

- *aMUSE*-ing Snacks: Get-Up-and-Go Gorp
- Dance Party
- Planning the Final Celebration
- Closing Ceremony: Thanking Our Bodies

Pages 70–71, girls' book

MATERIALS

- **Our Bodies: Beautiful and Strong:** 10–20 photos (from Web, magazines, etc.) of girls and women (not models) of varying sizes, shapes, ethnicities, and ages doing something active (playing a sport, dancing, cooking, gardening, on duty as a police officer or firefighter, leading an orchestra, or in other work situations)

- **Dancing Hands (option):** large, full-length mirror

- **Get-Up-and-Go Gorp:** muffin tins; small sandwich bags or paper cups; selection of nuts, seeds, dried fruits, etc. (see page 87)

- **Dance Party:** music CDs and CD player

- **Planning the Final Celebration:** large paper and easel, or chalkboard/whiteboard, and markers or chalk, or paper and pens

PREPARE AHEAD

Set up the CD player for the Dance Party.

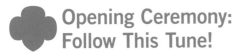
Opening Ceremony:
Follow This Tune!

Invite the girls to choose a song (or a verse of a song) they all know, and to take turns conducting or leading it. The first conductor moves her arms up and down as the other girls sing. The other girls watch her closely. When her arms are up, they sing fast. When her arms are down, they sing slowly. The conductor may signal to half the group to sing slowly while the other half sings fast.

Sharing Our Accessories

Gather the girls together and suggest that they strut down the runway with confidence, showing off the special accessory they are wearing. Then get a discussion going about their experiences trying the "Now, Head Out in a Hat or Scarf or . . ." activity in their books (page 69). You might ask:

- *Why did you choose to wear this particular accessory?*
- *Where did you wear it?*
- *How did it make you feel when you wore it?*
- *When you had it on, did you see yourself in a new way?*
- *Did wearing it boost your confidence?*
- *When you wore it again today, did you feel the same way?*
- *Will you wear it again? Why or why not?*

Our Bodies: Beautiful and Strong

Remind the girls of all that they've learned on this journey, by saying something like: *Now you know that women can take on any role they choose, and they do!* Then distribute the photos of girls and women in action and encourage the girls to discuss them. You might ask: *When you look at these photos, what do you notice first?*

chat time The girls might say, "They're all women!" Get them to think a little further by asking, "*What are they all doing that they might have in common?*" This might be a hard question at first, so you might prompt them by saying, "*They're all doing something. They're all being active!*"

Then ask:

- *We've spent a lot of time talking about the roles women and girls play in life. How do their bodies help them with those roles?*

- *Do you see how all the women's bodies in all these pictures are different, but all their bodies are helping them with what they are doing? (If a girl looks, for example, at the photo of a traffic officer, she might say, "Her body isn't helping her; she's just standing there directing traffic!" So say something like, "Look more closely! Stand up and try to do what she's doing. You need strength to hold your arm like that for that long.")*

- *How can you tell that the women in the pictures are confident?*

- *How do your bodies help you in all the roles you play every day?*

- *How do you feel about your body when you are running, playing soccer, dancing, or taking part in some other activity?*

- *What does your body do that makes you most proud?*

- *How do you thank your body for doing that? (Possible answers: By keeping it clean, giving it fresh air and healthful food and drink, listening to it when it's tired and giving it rest, and rewarding it from time to time, whether with favorite foods, activities, new adventures, or simple comforts, like sitting on a porch swing or lying in the grass.)*

Wrap up the discussion by letting the girls know that it's nice to be attractive, but most roles in life call for bodies that are healthy and skilled.

Option: Dancing Hands

Invite the girls to line up one behind the other, facing a large mirror. Have the girl in front hold her arms out to her sides, waving them up and down and moving her hands in various patterns, while holding the rest of her body still. The girls behind her hide their bodies behind hers, so only their arms and hands show. They wave their arms in patterns similar to the leader's to create a dance of gracefully moving arms and hands. The girls can take turns being first in line for this "hands dance."

aMUSE-ing Snacks

GET-UP-AND-GO GORP

Set out a selection of nuts and seeds, dried fruits, and other bite-size treats in the individual cups of muffin tins, and invite the Juniors to mix up their own versions of Gorp to enjoy during the Dance Party. Gorp is traditionally just good old-fashioned raisins and peanuts, but add in other treats that match the tastes and preferences of your group of Juniors (checking first for allergies).

Dance Party

Get out the music selections the girls decided on and get their Dance Party started by saying:

Some of best things we do in life are fun and healthy, and they let us thank our bodies without even thinking about it.

We walk to school with friends, go on a bike ride with our family, curl up with our dog for a nap, make a great dinner with an aunt.

Dancing together is also something fun and healthy that lets us thank our bodies. So, let's get up and dance, just like we planned.

Planning the Final Celebration

Let the girls know that the next time they get together will be a special celebration of all they've done along this journey. Take some time now for the girls to plan what they want to do, and to decide what role they will each play in executing the final celebration. Let the girls know that how the celebration rolls out is up to them! It might include:

- a special Girl-Led ceremony for receiving their final award, Try Out!
- sharing their commitments to continue trying on new roles in life
- any special invited guests
- a ceremonial passing of the Team Prop Box to a group of Brownies bridging to Juniors
- special music or songs
- themed snacks

Suggest that the girls first brainstorm together exactly what they would like this final journey celebration to be. This is also the time to set the date, time, and place, and create a guest list, if needed. Once the "big picture" view of the celebration is decided, the girls can divide into smaller teams that will cover all of the needed roles and duties to make the celebration a reality. The smaller teams might include:

Award ceremony team:
Two or three girls plan what will be said and done for the presentation of the Try Out! Awards. You might suggest that they return to the Team Prop Box one more time, and that the girls shout out "Bravas" to one another as they receive their awards.

Display/ decorations team:
Two girls might choose photos and materials that best highlight what the group accomplished along the journey. They might hang these on the wall or share them through a scrapbook that can be viewed at the celebration.

Snack team:
This team looks back on the journey's snacks and those featured in their book to select what to serve. Encourage them to consider the *amuse-bouche* recipes from chef Carla Hall that are featured in their book.

Invitations Team:
This team considers who will be invited and how to invite them, and also makes any needed invitations.

Clean-up team:
Remember, there are no small roles! This crew is very important. These girls might bring a few trash bags to the celebration and also a container to hold any recyclable items. They might also bring small plastic bags to pack up any leftover snacks so everyone can take some home.

When the teams huddle, guide them to organize what each team member will do, and then get going with it!

Closing Ceremony: Thanking Our Bodies

Gather the girls and say, *We just joined together to thank our bodies with a big Dance Party and a healthy snack. Now let's take turns saying one thing we will each do this week to show appreciation for our body.*

Looking Ahead to the Final Celebration

Check in with the girls and your Network to make sure all plans are on track. Remind the girls to bring their books because, at the Closing Ceremony, they'll double as autograph books that the girls will sign for one another.

FINAL CELEBRATION

Celebrating Me/Celebrating Us

MAKE THE MOST OF THE GIRLS' BOOK

The activities and discussions in this session correspond with "Inner Confidence, Outer Style" (pages 62–75) and "Muse-ing on Down the Road" (page 80) in the girls' book.

Pages 62–75, girls' book

AT A GLANCE

Goal: The Juniors celebrate their roles and their accomplishments along the journey and gain the courage to continue trying on new roles throughout life.

- Opening Ceremony: Roles We've Discovered for Ourselves

- Earning the Try Out! Award

- An *aMUSE*-ing Feast

- Looking Ahead: My Dream Role, My Story

- Closing Ceremony: Autographs All Around

MATERIALS

- **Earning the Try Out! Award:** awards for each Junior; Team Prop Box; and any other materials or equipment called for by the girls' celebration plans

- **An aMUSE-ing Feast:** *amuse-bouche* snacks (see page 63 in the girls' book) or another snack of the girls' choice

- **Closing Ceremony: Autographs All Around:** the girls' books, pens

PREPARE AHEAD

Check in with the girls that all plans are on track and that decorations and snacks are set up in time for the arrival of any guests.

 ### Opening Ceremony: Roles We've Discovered for Ourselves

Gather the girls together and ask them to take turns naming a role they now see for themselves that they never would have considered before this *aMUSE* journey they are now celebrating.

Earning the Try Out! Award

The girls receive their awards, according to the plans they've created. They start off by reaching into the Team Prop Box to select a prop at random to symbolize their promise and their courage to continue trying on new roles. You might say: *Now you have earned the Try Out! Award, which symbolizes that you have tried out new roles and promise to continue to use your confidence and courage to try out new roles throughout your life.*

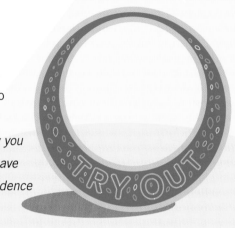

As each girl receives her award, the other girls and their guests shout out "Bravas!" in praise of her skills, qualities, new roles, and continued leadership.

NOW it's TiME to CELEBRATE!

An *aMUSE*-ing Feast

Serve the *amuse-bouche* snacks or any other snacks the girls have decided on, and celebrate!

Looking Ahead: My Dream Role, My Story

As the girls celebrate and enjoy their snacks, invite them to look ahead to new roles they might try in life and how these new roles will shape their life story. Ask:

What new roles do you dream of trying in your future years in Girl Scouts? In life? And how might these roles change your story? Do you want to:

- *take a new Girl Scout leadership journey?*

- *attend a Girl Scout camp?*

- *earn the Girl Scout Bronze Award?*

- *bridge to Cadettes and earn a LiA (Leader in Action) Award by assisting Brownies on their journey?*

- *travel via Girl Scout destinations?*

Closing Ceremony: Autographs All Around

Gather the girls together one last time and say something like:

- *Celebrities often autograph items for fans. Authors, for example, autograph their books.*

- *As you've taken on new roles in this journey, and promised to use your courage and confidence to take on new roles throughout your lives, you know you have a lot of fans, too—yourselves!*

- *You've cheered each other on through this journey, and today you shouted out "Bravas!" to one another.*

- *So take a few minutes now and autograph one another's books. Who knows? Someday you may be signing many more autographs for many more fans!*

- *Think about how great that will make you feel, and think how that may shape your story!*

Now, Give Yourself a Round of Applause

As the curtain comes down on *aMUSE*, take a moment to think about all that you have guided the Juniors to experience and accomplish along this journey. *Brava!* For the girls, this has been a wonderful journey of self-discovery and self-expression. It may have been one for you, too. So give yourself time to reflect on what the journey meant for you.

How has partnering with girls on this journey changed your story?

Have you tried out a new role or two along the way?

What have you learned about yourself, your skills, and your leadership qualities?

Has the journey changed your view of the roles open to women and girls, and the challenges they face as they take on new roles?

How does it feel to know you're part of the Girl Scout Mission to build girls of courage, confidence, and character, who make the world a better place?

What role do you hope to try next?

NATIONAL LEADERSHIP OUTCOMES

Every experience in this Junior *aMUSE!* journey
is designed to help girls be confident leaders
in their daily lives—and in the world!

Discover + Connect + Take Action = Leadership

DISCOVER

Girls understand themselves and their values
and use their knowledge and skills to explore the world.

	AT THE JUNIOR LEVEL, girls . . .	RELATED ACTIVITIES (by Session or girls' book chapter/activity)
Girls develop a strong sense of self.	are better able to recognize how situations, attitudes, and the behaviors of others affect their sense of self.	S2: Opening Ceremony, In the Classroom; S5: First, the Stereotype; S9: Closing Ceremon; S10: Sharing Our Accessories; Act 3: Confident, Stylish and Goofy, Head First, Now Head Out in a Hat or Scarf or, Listening to Your Inner Critic
	gain a clearer sense of their individual identities in relation to and apart from outside influences.	S1: Opening Ceremony, Closing Ceremony; S2: Opening Ceremony; S4: Ads Assume; S9: Opening Ceremony, Picture This, Mirror, Mirror, Closing Ceremony; S10: Sharing Our Accessories; Final Celebration: Opening Ceremony, Earning the Try Out! Award; GB: Act 1: Your Favorite Roles, All-My-Roles Paper Dolls; Act 2: Your Art, Your Part; Act 3: My Favorite Costume, Now Head Out in a Hat or Scarf or, Your Pin, Your Symbol
Girls gain practical life skills—girls practice healthy living.	gain greater understanding of what it means to be emotionally and physically healthy.	S10: A Show of Hands; Dance Party, Closing Ceremony; GB Act1: Acting Tip-Breathe, Acting Tip-Go Loosey-Goosey; GB Act 2: Green Goddess Dip, Listening to Your Inner Critic
	are more aware of family, cultural, and media influences on making healthy choices.	S2: Opening Ceremony; S4: Ads Assume; S9: Defining Real Beauty, Mirror, Mirror
Girls seek challenges in the world.	increasingly recognize that positive risk-taking is important to personal growth and leadership.	S1: Closing Ceremony; S8: Showtime, Closing Ceremony; Final Celebration: Earning the Try Out! Award; GB: Act 1: New Roles, New Records; Act 2: Your Heart, Your Art, Your Part
	are better at exploring new skills and ideas.	S2: Closing Ceremony; S3: Opening Ceremony, Casting Call Check-In; GB: Act 1: Storytelling with a Purpose, Stories Circle the Globe; Act 2: Your Heart, Your Art, Your Part; Act 3: Trading Roles
Girls develop critical thinking.	show greater skill in gathering and evaluating information.	S2: Logs and Leaders; S4: Ads Assume; S9: Defining Real Beauty; S10: A Show of Hands; GB: Act 1: Your Favorite Roles, Keep a Casting Call Log, Stereotype Tracker, Talk About Roles; Act 3: My Role Call Log, Trading Roles
	are better able to consider multiple perspectives on issues.	S2: Quick Draw, Quick Draw Part II; S4: Ads Assume; S5: First, the Stereotype; S9: Defining Real Beauty; GB: Act 1: Think Again, Talk About Roles

S=Session, GB=Girls' Book

CONNECT

Girls care about, inspire, and team with others locally and globally.

AT THE JUNIOR LEVEL, girls . . .		RELATED ACTIVITIES (by Session or girls' book chapter/activity)
Girls develop healthy relationships.	strengthen communication skills for maintaining healthy relationships.	S3: Closing Ceremony; S5: Agree to Disagree; GB Act 1: Talk About Roles, Keep a Casting Call Log
Girls promote cooperation and team building.	are better able to initiate and maintain cooperation on their teams.	S6&7: Opening Ceremony, What's My Role; S8: Showtime; S9: Opening Ceremony; S10: Planning the Final Celebration
Girls can resolve conflicts.	are better able to select conflict-resolution strategies to fit the situation.	S5: Agree to Disagree
Girls advance diversity in a multicultural world.	recognize the value of promoting diversity in the world.	S9: Defining Real Beauty; GB Act 1: Breaking the Mold
	develop a greater awareness of various forms of discrimination in the world.	S2: In the Classroom; S5: First, the Stereotype

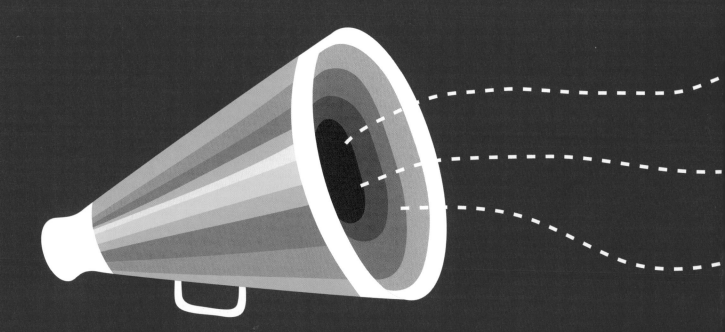

TAKE ACTION

Girls act to make the world a better place.

AT THE JUNIOR LEVEL, girls . . .	RELATED ACTIVITIES (by Session or girls' book chapter/activity)
Girls can identify community needs.	
strengthen their ability to decide which community issue deserves action.	S5: First, the Stereotype; GB Act 1: Stereotype Tracker, Think Again; GB Act 3: Award Tracker
begin to address deeper causes of issues in their communities.	GB Act3: Award Tracker
Girls are resourceful problem solvers.	
are able to create and implement detailed action plans for their projects.	S3: Planning Our Panel Discussion; S5: First, the Stereotype, Next, the Story Line, Tips for Creating a Story Line, Choosing Our Audience, Capturing Our Audience, Deciding How to Tell Our Story; S6&7: What's My Role; GB: Act 2: Think Like a Storyteller, Choosing Your Audience; Act 3: Award Tracker
increasingly seek out community support and resources to help achieve their goals.	S3: Reaching Out; GB Act 1: Talk About Roles; Act 2: Project Toolbox; Act 3: Award Tracker
Girls advocate for themselves and others.	
strengthen their abilities to effectively speak out or act for themselves or others.	S5: Choosing Our Audience, Capturing Our Audience, Deciding How to Tell Our Story; S6&7: What's My Role; S8: Showtime; Final Celebration: Opening Ceremony, Earning the Try Out! Award; GB Act 2: Storytelling with a Purpose, Choosing Your Audience
Girls educate and inspire others to act.	
learn various strategies to communicate and share Take Action Projects with others.	S5: Next, the Story Line, Tips for Creating a Story Line, Deciding How to Tell Our Story; GB Act 2: Storytelling with a Purpose, Your Heart, Your Art, Your Part, Think Like a Storyteller, Choosing Your Audience, Getting Your Audience on Its Feet
Girls feel empowered to make a difference.	
are more confident in their power to effect positive change.	S8: Showtime, Closing Ceremony, Final Celebration: Earning the Try Out! Award; GB Act 2: Give a Picture a New Story; Act 3: Award Tracker